Visitor
SOMERSE
& WIL

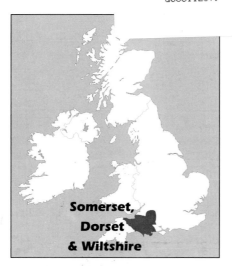

Somerset,
Dorset
& Wiltshire

VISITOR'S GUIDE

SOMERSET, DORSET & WILTSHIRE

Alan Proctor

MPC
HUNTER

Published by:
Moorland Publishing Co Ltd,
Moor Farm Road West, Ashbourne,
Derbyshire DE6 1HD England

ISBN 0 86190 574 1

Published in the USA by:
Hunter Publishing Inc,
300 Raritan Center Parkway, CN 94, Edison, NJ 08818

British Library Cataloguing in Publication Data:
A catalogue record for this book is available from the British Library.

Colour origination by: Scantrans, Singapore & GA Graphics, Stamford

Printed in Hong Kong by: Wing King Tong Co Ltd

Title page: Dorset Coast near Durdle Door (MPC Picture Collection)

Illustrations have been supplied by Alan Proctor: pages 19, 30, 31, 54, 70, 71, 74,
130, 139, 142, 146, 154, 160, 162, 163, 166, 167, 170, 179, 190, 191, 202, 203;
R. Sale 118-119; Ron Scholes: page 126; J. P. Walker pages 127, 131 (top).
All the remaining illustrations are from the MPC Picture Collection.

MPC Production Team:
Editorial & Design: John Robey
Cartography: Mark Titterton

Contents

Accommodation 214 • Archaeological & Historical Sites 214 • Climate 215 • Country Parks 216 • Craft Workshops 217 • Nature Reserves & Trails 217 • Opening Times • Transport 218 • Walking 218

KEY TO SYMBOLS USED IN TEXT MARGIN AND ON MAPS

✿	Garden	♉	Church/Ecclesiastical site
⌂	Castle/Fortification	⌘	Building of interest
✳	Other Place of Interest	⊓	Archaeological site
⇥	Nature reserve/Animal interest	⌂	Museum/Art Gallery
♣	Parkland	⚞	Recommended walk
⚘	Beautiful view/Scenery	⇛	Railway
⌶	Industrial Archaeology	✦	Birdlife
		⚲	Watersports

KEY TO MAPS

▭▭▭	Motorway	⣿⣿⣿	City/Town
▭▭▭	Main Road	◎ ◦	Town /Village
▭▭▭	Steam Railway	∿	River
▭▭▭	Canal	⬭	Lake/Reservoir
		⋯⋯	County Boundary

HOW TO USE THIS GUIDE

This MPC Visitor's Guide has been designed to be as easy to use as possible. Each chapter covers a region or itinerary in a natural progression which gives all the background information to help you enjoy your visit. MPC's distinctive margin symbols, the important places printed in bold and a comprehensive index enable the reader to find the most interesting places to visit with ease.

At the end of each chapter an Additional Information section gives specific details such as addresses and opening times, making this guide a complete sightseeing companion.

At the back of the guide the Fact File, arranged in alphabetical order, gives practical information and useful tips to help you plan your holiday before you go and while you are there.

The maps of each region show the main towns, villages, roads and places of interest, but are not designed as route maps and motorists should always use a good recommended road atlas.

Introduction

The unrivalled scenery of Somerset, Dorset and Wiltshire, which make up most of Wessex, makes these counties ideal holiday areas. Almost every type of landscape is here: perfect bays, coves and beaches, world-famous showplaces, pretty villages, historic towns and holiday resorts. No wonder the area tops the list for holidays.

Somerset is cider country, but the extensive cider apple orchards are only a part of the variations of scenery in this green and pleasant land. In the north the limestone Mendip Hills give way to the sea-level marshes of the 'moors' or levels. Sedgemoor is peaceful and tranquil now, but it has as remarkable a history as any region of Britain. History and legend are difficult to separate; the lines from the hymn 'And did those feet in ancient time walk upon Englands mountains green' is based on the supposition that Jesus may have visited here. Joseph of Arimathea, who was a trader and His uncle, is linked to the legend of the Holy Grail which King Arthur and his knights sought. King Alfred burnt the cakes at nearby Athelney. The last battle on English soil was fought at Sedgemoor.

Burnham-on-sea and Minehead are two fine resorts on the Bristol Channel coast, while the great landmark of Glastonbury Tor, overlooks the town. There are spectacular caves at Cheddar and Wookey, the great ecclesiastical houses of Wells Cathedral and Glastonbury Abbey, English wines to taste and buy — the list is almost endless. Not long ago, historically speaking, the great lowland areas were awash in winter leaving the higher ground as islands. It was the abbots of Glastonbury who started to drain the land. In the nineteenth century steam engines were used for pumping and some are now preserved and open as museums. At high tide the sea outside the walls at Highbridge seems higher than that of the great drains inside! Kings Sedgemoor drain, as it is unromantically called, is a haven for water fowl and fishermen alike.

The heartland of Somerset is the Vale of Taunton Dene. The lush green valley of the River Tone with its fertile meadows and orchards gives way towards the north-east to the Quantock Hills and then to Exmoor. From the highest point at Dunkery Beacon there are splendid views across the moor. Exmoor has a tiny church at Culbone, a remarkably well preserved clapper bridge at Tarr Steps, and the picturesque villages of Selworthy and Dunster. This is great walking country and tracks over the moor run for many miles. The South-West Peninsula Path starts at Minehead and the Severn to Solent Walk starts at Burnham-on-Sea.

Ancient hill forts abound in **Dorset**; Maiden Castle is the largest earthwork in Europe. The nearby county town of Dorchester, founded by the Romans, has a town trail which takes in some of its history. Dorset is Thomas Hardy country and the writer set his scenes in actual places. Jane Austen wrote *Persuasion* while living at Lyme Regis. History is all around, still to be seen. The Danes burnt Wareham, while Corfe Castle was a royal prison and the scene of a royal murder. Shaftesbury once had a great abbey, the remains of which can still be seen, while the steep cobbled Gold Hill is probably the most photographed street in England. The ancient hill figure of Cerne Abbas attracts much speculation and many visitors.

Along the rich coastline, from Bournemouth in the east, the scene could not be more varied with sandy sheltered beaches and charming small resorts. The ever popular Weymouth was a favourite of Charles II. Here there is a sheltered beach, pleasure craft harbour and a Channel Island rail-boat link. South is Thomas Hardy's

previous page: Lyme Regis

'Gibraltar Of Wessex' the Island of Portland. The great sweep of Chesil Beach eventually leads to the cliffs at Lyme Regis, a fossil hunter's paradise. In between is the small harbour of West Bay with Bridport a mile or so inland.

Wiltshire is a landlocked, inland county. It is rural England at its best. In the north-west it slides gently down to the meadowland along the Thames. From the Downs and forest near Marlborough the county undulates gently southwards to merge with Dorset at Cranborne Chase. Waves of corn sway in the breezes on the uplands round Salisbury Plain and the pure crystalline chalk streams flow through verdant valleys. Wiltshire has two Avon rivers: the 'Bath' Avon and the 'Hampshire' Avon, and even the mighty Thames graces the county for a few miles.

Wiltshire has unsurpassed countryside, with the great areas of rolling downland, country parks, forests and gardens, some of which are world-renowned. There is a rich heritage of over 4,500 ancient sites dating back to 4,000BC, including Stonehenge, Woodhenge, Avebury and Silbury. From the Beaker people to the Romans the remains are always interesting and often spectacular and are evidence of the attractiveness of the area to the early settlers.

The historic city of Salisbury is renowned for the soaring cathedral spire. At 125m (404ft) it is the tallest in England. The towns and villages are tiny time capsules of thatched or stone roofed weavers' cottages, with old lock-ups on village greens or old city gates. Some of the villages have magnificent old churches for quiet contemplation and some still have a traditional village green. Fascinating little market towns are dotted about the county: Devizes, which had a charter in 1141, or Chippenham, the village or *ham* of Cyppa the Saxon, which now has the largest cattle market in the south.

Wiltshire is also a watershed, the uplands of Salisbury Plain and, in the north, the Cotswolds, forming natural barriers. The Thames valley and the River Kennet, to the north of the area, flow in an easterly direction. The Salisbury Avon flows down through Hampshire to the south coast. The River Frome joins the Bath Avon to flow into the Severn Estuary beyond Bristol.

The great Ridgeway walk comes into the county near Liddington and extends to Lyme Regis in Dorset. An unofficial extension of the Ridgeway called The Wessex Way also crosses Wiltshire and Dorset to the south coast at Swanage. The Marlborough Downs offer fantastic walking country, as do the Downs to the south of Salisbury Plain. For those who prefer more secluded or sheltered walking there are many woodland walks.

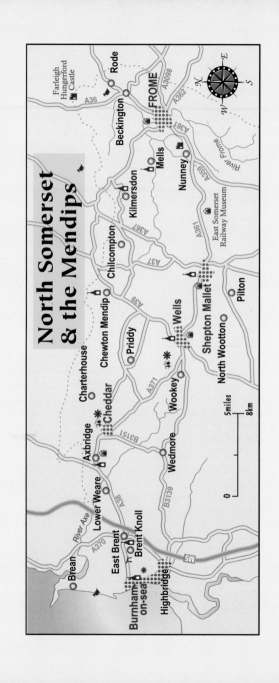

North Somerset
& the Mendips

North Somerset & the Mendips

1

This chapter deals with northern Somerset and a little of the county of Avon — green, gentle hills in the east and in the west the Mendip Hills with their steep escarpment to the south. To the north the slopes are gentle. To the south the escarpment gives way to the Somerset levels and 'moors'. Not moors in the sense of great heather covered uplands, these are low-lying marshy areas. The name Somerset was derived from an ancient tribe of people who came to the rich verdant areas with their cattle in the summer as summer settlers. In the winter they retreated to the hills as most of the area became waterlogged.

Four main roads go through this area, the A38 near the coast, the A39 from Bath to Wells with the A37 joining the A367 from Midsomer Norton to Shepton Mallet. Over on the eastern corner the A36 Bath to Salisbury road intercepts the A361 which goes to Frome and then on to Shepton Mallet. From Shepton Mallet the A371 goes to Wells, then along the foot of the Mendip escarpment. The many B roads that criss-cross the area give quieter motoring.

The first port of call is the Tropical Bird Gardens at **Rode**, just off the A36 about 4 miles north of Frome. In the 17 acres of garden, which were laid out many years ago, some of the birds fly free. It is a pleasant stroll round the gardens, visiting the aviaries which blend well with the surroundings. There are over a thousand birds of almost two hundred different species. A walk through the woods reveals ornamental pheasants and on the string of lakes water birds, including flamingoes and penguins. Children love the pets corner; there is also an aquarium and a butterfly and insect exhibition.

A little further south is the village of **Beckington**, which has some fine gabled and mullioned houses and a fine Norman church tower.

Only a few miles south is the delightful country town of **Frome**. The modern amenities of the town include bowls, tennis, fishing, a sports centre and an indoor swimming pool. This is a market town built on the steep banks of the River Frome, and near the town shopping centre there is a pleasant modern riverside terrace. Much of the centre of the town is a conservation area; not to be missed are Gentle Street with its old houses, and Cheap Street with the waterway running down the middle. The parish church is built on the site of a Saxon church.

Frome Museum has exhibits and records relating to the town and nearby villages. Historically, Frome was a woollen town, though this trade has long disappeared. The river in the lower town gave power for the mills and water for the dye houses. In the seventeenth century Judge Jeffreys had twelve men from the town hanged.

Just over a mile north of Frome are the gardens of Orchardleigh Park with a lake and an island church. They are only open on two days in the year, so enquire locally if intending to visit.

Vallis Vale, a mile to the west, is a lovely wooded walk along a deep valley. From Hapsford Mill along Mells River the vale turns south; the northern fork follows a path which leaves the river then rejoins it near Great Elm to continue to **Mells**, one of the loveliest villages in Somerset. In pre-Reformation times, this was the eastern outpost of Glastonbury Abbey's holdings. The pleasant stone cottages sit among gardens and trees around the splendid sixteenth-century Gothic church with a tower over 100ft high. It is a 3-mile walk back to Frome.

Just over 2 miles south of Mells lies **Nunney,** with remains of a fourteenth-century castle. The walls remain, with a cylindrical tower at each corner. A Parliamentary force bombarded the castle in

previous page: Nunney Castle

1645 and forced the Royalist defenders to surrender. The Parliamentarians then stripped the interior. Even the floor boards and joists went and the castle was never inhabited again.

About 7 miles north of Frome, by way of the A36 and then east along the A366 towards Trowbridge, is **Farleigh Hungerford Castle**. Building started in the late fourteenth century by Sir Thomas Hungerford, whose tomb can be seen in the chapel. Sir Thomas was the first speaker of the House of Commons. The castle replaced an older manor house. The castle chapel was the former village church, but it was incorporated into the castle and a new church was built for the villagers. Now in the care of English Heritage, the castle is sure of preservation.

Along the A366 back south-west to its junction with the A362, and straight across on the B3139 is **Kilmersdon.** Ammerdown House lies to the right and is a study centre for short special holidays with a specific purpose. The gardens are open on bank holidays only, and there are attractive walks in the extensive grounds.

Kilmersdon is worth a visit for the sake of the church, which dominates the small village and the valley.

The A361 leads towards Shepton Mallet. Some 8 miles along at a minor crossroads is a left turn to **West Cranmore**, the home of the East Somerset Railway Museum at Cranmore railway station. Here there is a standard gauge railway with its depot and signal box. There are six passenger coaches and seventeen wagons. The steam engine *Green Knight* is here and the star of the show, *Black Prince*, is the largest working steam locomotive in Britain.

Doulting is the next village towards Shepton Mallet and must be mentioned for its place in history. King Ine of Wessex gave the estate of Doulting to the monastery of Glastonbury in the eighth century. The gift was a memorial to the king's nephew St Aldhelm who died in the village. It was a valuable gift and remained with the abbey until the dissolution. The wealth of Doulting came mainly from great quarries to the north of the village where a creamy white stone was cut. Stone from here was taken to build Wells Cathedral, and was used for work on the abbey at Glastonbury. A great barn was built at the southern end of the village and this is now the main relic of a long Benedictine rule over the rich farmland estate.

Shepton Mallet is mentioned in the Domesday Book and Anglo-Saxon records date the origins of the town, but its rise to prosperity was through the weaving trade. As with so many other Somerset towns the weavers originally worked in their own cottages and sent their cloth for finishing to mills along the riverside. The church was

The Gothic church at Mells

Farleigh Hungerford Castle

built in the fifteenth century and has a fine tower and a splendid wagon roof. Built in 1500 and refurbished in 1841, the market cross is the centrepiece of the shopping area. The jail was built in 1624 and is still a jail, though the buildings in use now are modern; the last execution here was in 1926.

Shepton Mallet is the home of Showerings, the makers of Babycham. From humble beginnings as beer sellers, and later innkeepers, the firm grew to its present size. Myriads of the little bottles of this popular drink go out daily all over the country. Modern amenities in the town include bowls, tennis and an outdoor swimming pool. There is an eighteen-hole golf course just over a mile north of the town off the A37 Bristol road. A cinema also does duty as a theatre, and early closing day is Wednesday.

Almost 2 miles south, just off the A361, is the village of **Pilton**. At Pilton Manor Vineyard visitors can take a leisurely stroll and taste the wines. Across the main road and only a little over a mile away at **North Wootton** are Wootton Vines, another winery, where white wine and cider wine are made in traditional ways. Again visitors are welcome to walk in the vineyard. Geographically both these two villages are on the southern slopes of Mendip, giving the mild protected environment that the vines need. Vines were brought to England by the Romans, but it is only in recent years that the art has been seriously revived.

Wells can easily be reached from North Wootton by either of the roads going in a northerly direction. As Somerset's only cathedral city, Wells attracts many visitors; there is plenty to see in the city and around the area nearby.

Modern amenities are tennis, bowls, a heated open-air swimming pool and a nine-hole golf course. There is a theatre in town, and on the eastern outskirts a 3-mile nature trail starts from the market square; a guide leaflet is available from the curator of the museum. Blagdon Lake and Chew Valley Lake (both stocked with trout), are about ten miles from Wells in delightful scenery on the Mendip Hills. The panoramic view from the Pen Hill, near the television transmitter, takes in the fringes of Salisbury Plain to the east, while swinging westward the start of the Somerset marshes can be followed to the higher point of Glastonbury Tor. Far away to the west, if the light is right, there may be a glimmer of the sea at Bridgwater Bay. There is a nature trail at Pen Hill starting from near the transmitter, about 2½ miles long and with geological interest as well as plants and birds; a guide is available from the museum.

Regular walks are organized in the area, and the local information office will supply details. Visitors are always welcomed on the walks which are organised in many areas, often by the local branch of the Ramblers' Association. In the case of Wells, the Mendip Society organises regular walks in different areas of Mendip.

Lovers of history and historic buildings will find Wells a most beautiful cathedral city and a veritable treasure trove. The ubiquitous Romans seem to have bypassed Wells and King Ine of the West Saxons has first claim in the record books. He decided to build a church at this point where numerous springs rose from below the Mendips, hence the name of Wells. The cathedral dates from the twelfth century, but much extension and addition went on at least until the fifteenth century. There is much interesting glass in the cathedral dating from the fourteenth century. Over the High Altar the great east window is probably one of the finest of its kind in Britain. The great clock has an inner and outer dial showing the minutes and hours respectively. Phases of the moon are shown and at each quarter hour a tournament of knights takes place. The great clock was made about 1380, possibly at Glastonbury Abbey.

A unique picture is formed by the moated and fortified bishop's palace, one of the oldest inhabited houses in England. In the grounds are the famous springs from which Wells is named. The fortifications were added in the fourteenth century, the main buildings being a little older, when there were some differences of opinion with the townspeople. Though never actually needed at that time, the drawbridge was drawn up in 1831 when Reform Act rioters attacked the Bishop's Palace at Bristol.

Near the bridge, hanging low over the water just below a window, is a bell. The swans on the moat ring the bell to call for food. This practice is supposed to date back to Victorian times, but a piece of old glass at Nailsea Court suggests that the birds have been doing this little trick for much longer, possibly a few hundred years.

Among other interesting features of the city are the Bishop's Barn, dating from the fifteenth century, and St Cuthbert's Church, said to be the largest parish church in Somerset. Visitors approaching from Cheddar have been known to mistake this church for the cathedral. Llewellyn's Almshouses and the Old Deanery should also be seen along with the Chain Gate, Chapter House, Vicars Close, the Old Almshouses and Penniless Porch, where beggars used to gather to accost visitors to the cathedral.

The Cathedral Library, built about 1425, is partly open and treasures, manuscripts and books are on display. Wells Museum includes a collection of early Iron Age artifacts excavated from

Kilmersdon

Wookey Hole Cave, as well as pottery from various other Mendip caves. In one of the rooms is a fine collection of coins, minerals and local bird and animal life. There is an abundance of folk relics and a good collection of samplers.

A pleasant short walk starts from Moat Walk. At the end of the Walk go over a stile, cross the road to a wood and follow the winding path to the summit of Tor Hill, from where there is a charming view of the cathedral's east side.

There are many interesting houses and odd corners in the city that wait to be discovered, especially the sixteenth-century Crown Hotel

Wookey Hole paper mill

and the fourteenth-century bakery in St Thomas Street. New Street was once the haunt of Mendip miners when they came to town.

Wells is a good place from which to explore Mendip; being a 'tourist' city there is plenty of accommodation, yet it is small enough not to have major traffic problems.

Man has been around Mendip for centuries. A skeleton of a Palaeolithic man 12,000 years old was found in the Cheddar caves; his hunting ground was probably on Mendip.

Lead mines were being worked on Mendip before the Roman invasion, as fishermen down on the lower ground used lead weights in prehistoric times. Charterhouse was the centre of mining for the Romans. Only six years elapsed between the first landing of the Romans and the full operation of the mines. Two pigs of lead have been found stamped with a name, enabling accurate dating. Silver was also found and some British states had a silver coinage. Some of the lead no doubt went to Bath where lead pipes still carry water to and from the Roman Baths.

There is ample evidence that the Saxons used lead for church roofs, but there is no further evidence for the working of the mines until the twelfth century when the Bishop of Bath was granted a mining charter by Richard I. Mining went on through the Middle Ages, right up till the first half of the nineteenth century. However, by the end of the seventeenth century, the easily accessible deposits had been worked out, the miners had to go deeper and often ran into trouble with flooding.

Other minerals, such as ores of zinc, manganese and iron, were also mined as early as the thirteenth century. Very little is known about the life the miners led. Among the first to record details of the miners' lives were Hannah More and her sister Martha. Hannah devoted herself to improving the lot of the poor. The miners were recorded as having been 'savage, depraved, brutal and ferocious'. No policeman would dare to attempt to arrest a Shipham man, as he would have feared for his life.

The core of the Mendips is carboniferous limestone, a rock that dissolves easily in the small amount of carbonic acid in rainwater. Water either seeping down or welling up chooses the weaker spots, seeping into the cracks which become fissures, which in turn become channels and caves, and eventually the glorious caverns at Wookey Hole and Cheddar.

The surface plateau, in medieval times, was a royal Forest in the sense that it was a hunting ground or chase. On the site of an ancient Saxon hunting lodge at Axbridge there is a house dating from the sixteenth century, named King John's Hunting Lodge. It is now a National Trust property and is open as a museum.

Monks of the Carthusian order, who gave Charterhouse its name, developed sheep farming and the wool trade — though goats are recorded in the Domesday Book, fifty goats at Chewton Mendip and sixty-eight at Rodney Stoke. In times of necessity, such as World War II, arable farming was substituted and barley and potatoes were grown. When that necessity receded the farmers went back to sheep, for arable farming is a little precarious on the misty, wind- and rain-swept heights.

Priddy, with its stone circles and barrows, retains the atmosphere of the sheep farming community. There is a stack of hurdles reputed to have stood on the green for three hundred years. Priddy Sheep Fair has been an annual event for many years where the traditions of sheep buying and selling and hiring of staff take place. The Fair still takes place on 18 August every year.

Wookey Hole is 2 miles away from Wells, and here visitors can see the Great Cave with its different chambers and the legend of the Witch of Wookey. There is Britain's last handmade paper mill, and an exhibition of fairground figures. About a mile to the north-west of the village is the Ebbor Gorge national nature reserve. Starting from the car park at Deer Leap Road there are two trails. The shortest is half a mile long, passing through quiet woodland. The second trail is 1½ miles and is a more strenuous walk passing through a rugged gorge and grassland. Another trail, the Moors Trail, starts from **Easton** village by the church, just off the Wells to Cheddar road. This trail runs for 4 miles, and a leaflet is available from Wells Museum. The trail traverses a typical section of Somerset level or moor.

Following the A371 north-west leads to **Cheddar**, famous for giving its name to Cheddar cheese. William Camden, writing in the sixteenth century, said that 'it was famous for the excellent and prodigious great cheeses made there'. Nowadays, of course, Cheddar-type cheeses may come from New Zealand. Daniel Defoe wrote in 1722 that 'The whole village were cow keepers'. Cheddar is now almost as famous for its strawberries as for its caves. The sloping fields between the main road and the hills are well sheltered from the cold north wind and early vegetables as well as strawberries are grown in profusion.

The Celtic belief that some hills were filled with passages in an underground fairy world is understandable after a visit to the Cheddar caves. The glistening colourful rocks often give dramatic

Cycle racing through Cheddar Gorge

effects, and the delicate shading is not caused by the lighting, but by the various minerals in those rocks. Formations have been given names, delightfully descriptive, such as Fairy Grotto, Frozen River and many more. The caves were used as human habitation for many years, and in the museum there is a life-size display of Palaeolithic man. This first recorded use of the caves dates from 10,000 years ago. In the Dark Ages the caves were used as a refuge by the Romano-British during the fifth and sixth centuries. Many Roman coins, along with weapons and domestic articles, have been found.

These caverns are still not fully explored and most weekends will see the cavers in action. Many caving clubs operate in the region, exploring and searching for new routes. However, the Mendip Rescue Organization does not exist for nothing. Deaths have occurred in the caves, mostly of inexperienced amateurs without proper equipment, or people who are trapped by rising waters. Sudden flooding is just one of the hazards, for a summer storm may cause the waters to rise rapidly. So be warned, if you wish to go caving join a club and get expert advice and help. Caves open to the public are, of course, perfectly safe.

The two main caves at Cheddar, Gough's and Cox's, were discovered in the nineteenth century. Cox was a miller digging at the rockface to make room for a new shed when he found his cave. Though Gough's cave was known earlier, Mr Gough and his sons did a tremendous amount of work in making the passages safe for visitors. One may now stroll on smooth paths, conducted by a knowledgeable guide, without even getting dirty shoes.

For a breathtaking view (and a breathtaking climb) take the 322 steps of Jacob's Ladder up the side of the gorge. The splendid view of the Somerset moors, to the Quantocks and Exmoor, makes the climb well worth the effort. A whole day can easily be spent in the gorge, with Jacob's Ladder, the caves, refreshments, or a full meal in one of the restaurants, as well as the exhibition and museum. The gorge is also the starting point for many walks with some delightful picnicking spots. One may even be able to watch some of the many rock climbers on Cheddar Cliffs. In some places the walls of the gorge rise nearly 500ft.

Higher up the gorge is the Black Rock Nature Trail. The start is about 1½ miles north of Cheddar, up the gorge, in Black Rock Drive. It is 2 miles long and is a woodland walk with good views over the Mendip countryside.

Charterhouse, 2 miles north-east from Cheddar, was the main Roman lead mining area and many Roman coins have been found in the vicinity. Traces of the workings remain in the fields. From the minor road just north of the church, a bridleway leads up to Mendip's highest point — Beacon Batch on Black Down is 325m (1,067ft) high with splendid views and is only slightly lower than the highest point of the Cotswolds. It is possible to walk on down to Cheddar, or to turn north and go down to Burrington Combe.

The deep cut Burrington Combe carries the B3134 down off the plateau to join the A368. Although it is not as spectacular or as deep as Cheddar Gorge, it has its place in history. It was in the combe in 1762 that the Rev Augustus Toplady, a curate of Blagdon, took advantage of a cleft in the rocks to shelter from a storm. While sheltering here he got the idea for his hymn 'Rock of Ages' and a carved inscription records the fact.

Lovers of churches should visit St Mary Magdalene at Chewton Mendip, east of Cheddar, and Axbridge church to the west. **Chewton Mendip** church, which is fifteenth century, has one of those splendid towers, while **Axbridge** has some good glass and brasses. Also in Axbridge is the National Trust property known as King John's Hunting Lodge. The house was built about 1500 and is an example of the rising prosperity of the merchants of the times. It is now a museum with changing exhibits.

From the church at Axbridge there is a walk south-east to the reservoir. Join a track and turn right; cross the River Yeo and go downstream to recross at the first bridge and head back to the church, about 3½ miles for the round trip.

On the A38, a mile south-west from Axbridge, is Lower Weare and a further 3 miles along the A38, just after crossing the M5, is a minor road to East Brent. Brent Knoll was almost certainly an island long ago, before the levels were drained. It rises to 137m (450ft) and is topped by an Iron Age hillfort; it is a conspicuous landmark from miles around and can be seen from South Wales. There is a footpath to the top from a point close to East Brent church.

The villages of Brent Knoll, or South Brent and East Brent, both have churches with interesting features. On the south-western slopes of the hill the church of **Brent Knoll** has an interesting series of bench ends, which tell the story of a parish priest of long ago who had a quarrel with the abbot of Glastonbury. Both villages were part of the ecclesiastical estates, and surprisingly the priest won. The carvings commemorate the victory: the abbot is shown as a fox and the parishioners as various animals including geese. In the final scene the abbot is hanged by the geese. **East Brent** church has a fine plaster ceiling dating from the early part of the seventeenth century. There are also some carved bench ends in the nave, including the arms of the abbey as well as the initials of Abbot Selwood.

Brent Knoll is only a few miles from the sea and the road north through Berrow passes camping and caravan sites and access points to **Brean** sands. At the far end rises Brean Down. This is really an outcrop of the Mendips and gives a fine clifftop walk of a mile or so with exhilarating sea breezes and wide views. The top is springy turf and the whole of the Down is a National Trust property and a nature reserve. There is a tropical bird garden near Brean with many exotic birds on show.

South of Berrow is **Burnham-on-Sea**, which has developed from a centre of early agricultural improvement to a resort and spa. The town also had a place in railway and shipping development. Burnham's only medieval relic is the church; the west tower leans, no doubt due to the shifting sands below. A fine Jacobean pulpit and a Georgian chandelier, the latter made by a brass founder of Bridgwater named Bayley, are among its features. The sculptures now at Burnham once formed part of the baroque altarpiece of the Gothic chapel at Whitehall Palace.

A curate of the parish, the Rev David Davies, helped the advance of Burnham-on-Sea by digging wells from which he hoped to get waters similar to those discovered at Cheltenham. Both saline-chalybeate and sulphurous waters were found; they met with a mixed reception but the birth of the town as a resort was assured.

The Rev Davies was also interested in lighthouses. Burnham overlooks the once busy sea approaches to Bridgwater and Highbridge. The enterprising curate built a new lighthouse and secured an Act of Parliament under which he could levy tolls on passing ships. Trinity House later took over the sea lanes and in 1832 a new lighthouse was built.

Modern facilities include an eighteen-hole golf course, where the West of England Open Championship is held; it lies to the north of the town between Berrow and the sea. Burnham has an indoor swimming pool and facilities for bowls, tennis, boating and fishing.

A walk along the Esplanade leads to **Highbridge**, which was once a busy port. The bridge that gave the town its name was in reality a dam. At high tides the water on the seaward side was higher than the river. The heyday of the port was in the eighteenth and nineteenth centuries, and movement of goods was greatly helped by the Glastonbury Canal which opened in 1833. Railways superseded the canal in 1854, backed by the shoemakers Clarks of Street, who wanted better transport for their growing business.

The Somerset and Dorset Railway (the old S and D was affectionately known as 'slow and dirty') repaired engines at High-bridge well into the twentieth century. Local business interests helped the docks to expand, they even survived the withdrawal of the railway interest in the 1930s. The port remained working up to 1948, but although it is now almost derelict it is still interesting.

Additional Information

Accommodation
£££ = expensive
££ = moderate
£ = inexpensive
EM = evening meal available

Burnham-on-Sea
Sandhills Guest House (££, EM)
3 Poplar Road, TA8 2HD
☎ 01278 781208

Priors Mead (£)
23 Rectory Road, TA8 2BZ
☎ 01278 782116
Food available in the town.

Cheddar
Gordons Hotel (£)
Cliff Street, BS27 3PT
☎ 01934 742497

Tor Farm (£, EM)
Nyland, BS27 3UD
☎ 01934 743710

Frome
Mendip Lodge Hotel (£££, EM)
Bath Road, BA11 2HP
☎ 01373 463223

Shepton Mallet
Hurlingpot Farm (£)
Chelynch, Doulting, BA4 4PY
☎ 01749 880256
Food available at the Poacher's
Pocket, Doulting.

Wells
Ancient Gate House Hotel (££, EM)
20 Sadler Street, BA5 2RR
☎ 01749 672029

Fenny Castle House (£)
Fenny Castle, Wookey, BA5 1NN
☎ 01749 672265

Places to Visit

Axbridge
Axbridge Museum (NT)
King John's Hunting Lodge
The Square, BS26 2AP
☎ 01934 732012
Open: Easter-September daily 2-5pm.

Burnham-on-Sea
Brean Tropical Bird Gardens
To the north at Steart Flats.
Open: daily April-October.

Cheddar
Cheddar Caves
☎ 01934 742343
Open: daily all year.

Frome
East Somerset Railway
☎ 01749 880417
Open: daily March-October, weekends only Nov-March 9am-4pm.

Farleigh Hungerford Castle
☎ 01225 754026
Open: April-September daily
10am-6pm, October daily 10am-
4pm, November-March Wednesday-Sunday 10am-4pm.

Frome Museum
Open: March-November, Wednesday, Friday and Saturday.

Nunney Castle
Nunney
Open: daily all year.

Rode Bird Gardens
☎ 01373 830326.
Open: daily 10am-6pm in summer
and 10am to sunset in winter.

Shepton Mallet
Shepton Mallet Museum
Exhibits from the Mendips.
☎ 01749 72552 (Wells Information
Office) for opening times.

Wells
Wells Museum
☎ 01749 673477
Open: Wednesday-Sunday
November-Easter 11am-4pm, Easter-
June, September-October 10am-
5.30pm, July & August 10am-8pm

Wookey Hole
☎ 01749 672243
Open: daily except 25 December,
summer 9.30am-5.30pm, winter
10.30am-4.30pm.

Tourist Information Centres

Axbridge (Somerset Visitor Centre)
Sedgemoor Services, M5 South
☎ 01934 750833

Burnham-on-Sea
South Espanade
☎ 01278 787852

Cheddar
The Cliff (Sundays only in winter)
☎ 01934 744071

Frome
The Round Tower, Bridge Street
☎ 01373 467275

Shepton Mallet (open summer only)
☎ 01749 345258

Wells
Town Hall, Market Place
☎ 01749 672552

With the licensing of England's first full cider distillery, the craft of distilling is being revived again in the orchards of Somerset

Central Somerset

2

From the eastern part of the county, where the gentle hills roll down from Wiltshire, the land drops down to the Somerset levels or moors. The levels are divided roughly by the Polden Hills. From Shepton Mallet the A361 goes to Glastonbury and on to Taunton. Coming from Wells the A39 goes through to Bridgwater. Both these routes follow what high ground there is and from Glastonbury to Bridgwater the A39 runs along the top of the Poldens. In the old days the levels in winter were often flooded and large shallow lakes appeared, so any travelling had to be along higher ground. The monks of Glastonbury were largely responsible for the countryside looking as it is now, when they started draining the moors.

Driving south on the B3092, a west turn on the A303 leads to **Wincanton**. Fortunately the town itself is bypassed, so it is fairly quiet. It is a thriving market town surrounded by rich pastureland, and has some interesting buildings. As it is almost exactly midway between London and Plymouth, at one time it was a re-mounting point for couriers and later became an important staging post for coaches on their way to and from the west. As many as seventeen coaches a day stopped in the coaching heyday.

The parish church dates from the fourteenth century, but it was rebuilt in 1889. There is a medieval carving of St Eligius in the north porch, while in the churchyard is a monument to Nathaniel Ireson, one of the town's most notable men, who had a hand in much local building.

From the village of **Cucklington**, about 3 miles south-east, there is a fine ridge walk of a mile, north from the church, giving good views over the surrounding countryside. From the local tourist information office a leaflet can be obtained giving directions for a circular 'Wincanton Walk' about 3 miles long.

On the way north from Wincanton on the B3081 towards Bruton is Redlynch Lake, set in superb countryside and with some very good fishing. 3kg (7lb) carp and 2kg (4lb) tench can be taken. Details are available from the Tourist Information Office in Wincanton.

Bruton is a small town, but like so much of this area it has its place in history. Berkeley Square in London is named after the first Baron Berkeley who invested in what was then open land. The baron's home town is also commemorated in London by Bruton Street. When Henry VIII dissolved the monasteries one of the lucky Somerset families were the Berkeleys. The king's standard bearer at that time was Sir Maurice Berkeley, and he was given the abbey at Bruton and its lands. The first baron was ennobled for his services to the Royalist cause during the Civil War. Tombs of the Berkeley family can be seen in Bruton church.

The town had one of the first fulling mills in England, built about 1290. Another famous son of the town, who started life as a stable boy, was Hugh Sexey, who made good and eventually founded the famous Sexey's School.

Bruton is one of the gems of the quiet Somerset country — the splendid Gothic parish church, the almshouses, the pack horse bridge and the dovecote make this historic small town well worth a visit. The dovecote is National Trust and is a sixteenth-century roofless type standing about half a mile south of the town centre.

Down the A359 about 4 miles south-west is Hadspen House, where the ornamental gardens are open. A turn up the A371 leads to **Castle Cary**. The best surviving feature here is the old lockup which

---

previous page: A vintage cider brandy still at Kingsbury Episcopi

was built in 1779 and is only 7ft diameter. It has a pagoda-like roof. There is a small museum in the town which is worth visiting.

South from Castle Cary is **South Cadbury** and Cadbury Castle, a claimant to the title of Camelot, and probably a stronger one than the Cornish claim as the site of Arthur's last battle. The wounded Arthur was taken to Glastonbury, a long way from Cornwall, but only 15 miles from Cadbury and at one time joined to it by a track. After Arthur's death Guinevere took holy vows and later became Abbess of Amesbury. When she died Lancelot took her body to Glastonbury, the *Avalon* of legend, and buried her beside Arthur.

Cadbury Castle is one of the greatest hillforts in southern Britain. A walk round the mighty ramparts is almost a mile. Traces of Neolithic, Bronze Age and Iron Age use have been found here and after the Roman legions departed it was refortified and used by the Romano-British. This was about AD500, possibly its Arthurian period. Later, about AD1000, it was again refortified by Ethelred the Unready for defence against the Danes. A mint was established here and much of the coinage was used to pay off the Danes (*Danegeld* as it was called). Most of the surviving Cadbury coins now lie in Scandinavian museums. The views from the walk round the ramparts reveal the scope of this place as a defensive site, movements to the north and west would have been spotted in plenty of time to get organised. The important route of the Fosse Way is clearly visible.

Only 6 miles along the main A303 is the Fleet Air Arm Museum at **Yeovilton**. The museum shows the early development of naval flying from its origins in 1910 to the present. Concorde 002 is also on display and a visit will take up most of a day.

Just north of the Fleet Air Arm Museum, a little way up the minor road to Charlton Mackerell, is Lyte's Cary. This typical Somerset manor house was the home of the Lyte Family for five hundred years. The great hall is fifteenth century with later additions including the sixteenth-century great chamber. There is a fourteenth-century chapel. Probably the best known member of the Lyte family was the Elizabethan Sir Henry Lyte, who wrote a standard work on horticulture. The gardens date from that time.

Almost opposite the drive to Lyte's Cary is a minor road to **Kingsdon**, a quiet village with a fifteenth-century church in among the cottages. The church houses the stone figure of a knight who ruled Kingsdon in the thirteenth century when Edward III was king.

Somerton is just under 3 miles along the B3151. Somerton was once an important town, not only to Somerset but to all of Wessex. To its good fortune it has been bypassed by the modern world. Here

Castle Cary museum

is the delightful Broad Street, the old town hall, some excellent
Georgian houses and a medieval market cross built during the reign
of Charles II. It was a royal manor and a castle superseded the
original Saxon fort. The castle does not appear to have been used as
a fortress after the reign of Henry III, but was probably used as a jail.
It is believed that the White Hart inn covers part of the site. The
church, which is near the market cross, has a transeptal southern
tower. Royal control must have been the key to the long survival of
what is now a delightful little town.

For an energetic 7-mile walk start from Somerton and go north to
Etsome Farm, then cross the River Cary. Keep going north by a
track, then a footpath to Dundon. Take the footpath round Dundon
Hill with extensive views over the surrounding moors and hills.
From Hayes Farm go south to join a minor road and back to Somerton.

Alternatively from Dundon keep going north to cross another
stretch of moor and pass Ivy Thorn Manor to climb up Ivy Thorn
Hill near the Youth Hostel. Turn left by the road, which for most of
the way is unfenced so that it is possible to walk through the trees.
Continue to Walton Hill and turn left on a footpath just past the
windmill. Near the bottom of the hill meet the road at the top of a T-
junction. Go south-west down the road for a quarter of a mile and

Somerton: the church (top) and market cross

straight on down a track where the road goes right. Cross Eighteen Feet Rhyne and Somerton Moor, then join and follow the minor road back to Somerton. This is a round trip of about 14 miles. Ivy Thorn Hill and Walton Hill are National Trust properties, the total area being just under 90 acres, and there are some good viewpoints from here to both sides of the hills.

Just to the east is the village of **Butleigh**, which was the home of the Hood family. On the great hill nearby is the Hood monument. Admiral Hood died in 1814, and the towering column was erected by his officers to his memory.

West of Somerton a minor road branches off the B3153 just on the town outskirts to **High Ham** where there is the last thatched windmill in England. It dates from 1822 and was working until 1910.

High Ham is on a rocky peninsula looking over the moors to the north, while a narrow pass to the south is guarded by Langport. The River Parrett passes through this gap on its way to Bridgwater. The other side of Langport is a long narrow peninsula with Curry Rivel at its north-western end. Over these long extensions of the moors meander the Rivers Yeo (or Ivel) and Isle to join the Parrett at Langport, and then only a few miles downstream the River Tone joins near Burrow Bridge.

A study of detailed maps of the area shows that the lower-lying areas such as the wide stream valleys south of Langport, and West Sedge Moor, north-west of Curry Rivel, have no buildings. This is further evidence of the floods of years ago. There was little point in building a barn if the food stored in it was ruined by winter floods, so all the buildings were built on the higher ground. Much of West Sedge Moor even here, 15 miles from the sea, is only 5m (16ft) above sea level. The River Parrett near Langport is about the same level, so the rivers are sluggish and slow to drain the surrounding land.

About 2 miles south of Langport are the ruins of **Muchelney Abbey**. The abbey was founded in 939 by the Benedictines and was an important ecclesiastical establishment, though not as large as Glastonbury. During the Dissolution the abbey escaped immediate destruction, but gradually sank into decay. In the tiny village the church and cottages contain some pieces salvaged from the abbey.

While in this area you can sample the brandy distilled from cider by the Somerset Cider Brandy Company at Kingsbury Episcopi.

West across the River Parrett from Muchelney is the village of **Drayton**, and Midelney Manor. The sixteenth-century manor house was once part of the abbey estates and since the dissolution has been the property of the Trevilian family. There are the very interesting falconer's mews to be seen, as well as the gardens and a heronry.

Curry Rivel is under a mile away and straddles the A378. A recommended walk is west from the church along a minor road, which soon turns north. At a T-junction go straight ahead on a track, take the first left and at the end of the track go north to the woods, then swing left in a large loop to the road at Heale and so back to the start. This 2-mile walk has good views over West Sedge Moor from near the summit of Red Hill.

Langport church is worth visiting; there is some fine stained glass and among the saints depicted is Joseph of Arimathea. The Hanging Chapel has no connection with Judge Jeffreys's rampage through the west country as might be supposed. The term hanging refers to the fact that it once perched on top of the town gate and now seems to hang in the air. It was built in 1353 and the chapel served as a merchant guild before having a spell as town hall.

Langport has been identified by scholars as *Llongborth*, and if this is correct then the town existed in the sixth century. There is a reference, in an ancient Welsh book, to a battle fought here by Geraint in the time of King Arthur. Geraint was king of the Dumnonii, the tribe occupying the area before the Roman invasion. The town was important enough to have had a mint for a long time. The fact that the River Parrett could be forded here made it an ideal place for a town. In the thirteenth century an imposing stone bridge with nine arches, and called Great Bow, was built here. All the houses in Bow Street lean backwards, the fronts having better foundations than the back. The great bridge was pulled down in 1840 to make way for river traffic at a period when Langport had some prosperity as a port. River traffic took goods to Ilchester and Yeovil.

There are some good riverside walks along the river banks from Langport. One suggested route is east along the north bank. Change sides at the first bridge and go south to Muchelney to view the abbey ruins before walking back again, to make a 4-mile round trip.

From Langport a minor road leads to **Burrow Bridge** and the Aller Moor Pumping Station, one of the stations which helped keep the moors drained. Among the exhibits are three huge steam engines and pumps built by Easton and Amos in the 1860s. Nearby is Burrow Mount or Burrow Mump, which is reputedly the site of King Alfred's island refuge from the Danes when his fortunes were at a low ebb. The 9½-acre National Trust site has an unfinished eighteenth-century chapel on the summit. This chapel is on the site of an earlier one and it was once the site of a Norman fort.

About 2 miles south is **Stoke St Gregory**, where the ancient art, or craft, of willow weaving may be examined. Withy, as the locals call it, has been used for centuries for basket making and still survives. The harvest of willow is still taken from this fast growing wetland tree. At Meare Green Court is the Willows and Wetland Visitor Centre with a wetland exhibition, a guided tour of the willow

The National Trust
**STEMBRIDGE
TOWER MILL**
OPEN APRIL–SEPTEMBER
SUNDAYS & BANK HOLIDAY
MONDAYS 2.30-5.30
for by price appointment with the tenant
ADMISSION £x.xx
Dogs are not permitted

The thatched windmill at High Ham

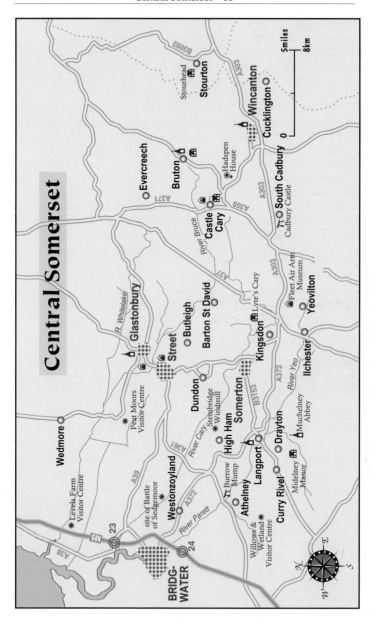

Central Somerset

Stourhead
Stourton
Wincanton
Cucklington
B3092
A303

Evercreech
Bruton
Hadspen House
A371
Castle Cary
South Cadbury
Cadbury Castle
A359
River Bruce
A37

Glastonbury
R. Whitelake
Butleigh
Barton St David
Lyte's Cary
Kingsdon
Fleet Air Arm Museum
Yeovilton
Street
Dundon
Somerton
Ilchester
Stembridge Windmill
River Cary
A372
River Yeo
A303

Peat Moors Visitor Centre
High Ham
Langport
Drayton
Muchelney Abbey
B3153

Wedmore
Levels Farm Visitor Centre
A39
site of Battle of Sedgemoor
Burrow Mump
Atheley
Curry Rivel
Midelney Manor
A361
A372
River Parrett

Westonzoyland
Willows & Wetland Visitor Centre

BRIDG-WATER
M5
23
24
A38

5 miles
8 km
0

N
S
E
W

industry, the willow trail (a walk to the withy beds), talks on the industry and a weaving shed. There is also an RSPB display.

Due north by way of quiet minor roads is **Westonzoyland**. Here is another pumping station with an 1861 Easton and Amos steam pump and other items of interest from the days of steam-powered drainage. There is also a working blacksmith's forge.

Westonzoyland is famous, or infamous, as the place where the captured rebels were brought after the Battle of Sedgemoor in 1685. The parish register gives the beginning of the sad tale of vengeance. About five hundred prisoners from the battle were taken into the church. Twenty-two were hanged at once, four of them in chains. Colonel Kirke, one of the Royalist officers, set out on a ruthless rounding up of suspected rebel sympathisers. One family had an elderly lady hauled away merely for rendering help to an injured man. In another family when the suspect was not found his brother was taken in his place. Colonel Kirke is reputed to have stated that it was the family that owed a life. Eventually over a thousand prisoners were held in various jails throughout the West Country. Five hundred people were condemned in both Taunton and Wells — the five hundred in Wells in only a single day! Many were hanged, drawn and quartered, then the remains were boiled in salt and preserved with pitch. The executions were public and the preserved remains were put on public display, often outside the victim's own house. To take the body down was an offence punishable by a period in the pillory. Many were transported to the West Indies to serve as slaves in the canefields including many who had been condemned to death. Some died on the trip out, some died due to the hard labour of the fields.

In 1688 another rebellion took place, this time successful, when William III landed with a large army, and James II fled without a fight. The convicted rebels were reprieved and many returned to their homes.

Continue north to East Huntspill on the B3141, then by way of a minor road through **Hackness** to the Levels Farm Visitor Centre at the 300-year-old New Road Farm. This a typical mixed low-level farm with lots of different animals, a nature trail, farm shop and plant sales, machinery, and a picnic site. There is a daily milking demonstration, with hay making, sheep shearing and incubation.

The main road allows a speedy passage up to Street and Glastonbury. At one time **Glastonbury** may have been an island, or at least a peninsula and access was difficult, particularly in winter. Small boats sailed up the river; Joseph of Arimathea is said to have 'landed' and implanted his staff, which grew into the celebrated Christmas flowering Glastonbury Thorn.

Evidence of early occupation is ample and mysterious. Prehistoric occupation took place both on the Tor and on and around the lakes. Joseph and his eleven disciples landed one Christmas morning about AD30, and built the first church, of wattle and daub, on the site of the present abbey ruins. The Romans grew vines on the southern slopes. King Ine built the first monastery in 688 and legend links St Patrick with Glastonbury. King Arthur, and later Queen Guinevere, were reputedly buried here. The Chalice Well is linked with the Arthurian legends and the quest for the Holy Grail. It also has an ancient tradition of healing and in the eighteenth century this gave the town some reputation as a spa.

St Dunstan, who later became Archbishop of Canterbury, introduced Benedictine rule and from his appointment seems to stem the rise of the wealth and influence of the abbey.

One of the mysteries of the area and difficult to see except from the air, is the Glastonbury Zodiac. A circle 15 miles across and centred on Butleigh, it has the signs of the zodiac as raised ridges on the ground. Why, how, or by whom it was created no one knows.

Glastonbury Tor is a conical hill with a tower, the remains of a church, on the top. The Tor and St Michael's Tower dominate the surrounding countryside, and give superb views from the top.

Glastonbury has much to see. There are old houses worth looking at, and the churches are full of interest. The abbey ruins are, of course, the prime tourist attraction, but the dedicated will also want to see the Abbey Barn, built in the fourteenth century, which is now the home of the Somerset Rural Life Museum. The exhibits include hand tools and horse-age machinery, rural crafts, wheelwright's shop, cider making and peat digging. The Tribunal, a medieval courthouse dating back to 1400 where the abbots had considerable influence, is also a museum.

Chalice Well, or blood spring, lies at the foot of the Tor. Early Christian and Arthurian legend links it with healing and the quest for the Holy Grail. It is open all year, but afternoons only in winter.

The façade of the George and Pilgrims Hotel is regarded as one of the finest panelled designs and the hotel is a good example of an original inn. Founded between 1327 and 1377 it was rebuilt about 1460 and has offered accommodation to pilgrims ever since.

Irregular mounds seen from the Godney road just outside town, are the site of a prehistoric lake village discovered in 1892. Probably dating from 150BC the village was built on platforms above the

Burrow Mump

The Somerset Levels

swamps. Artifacts from the excavations are in the Tribunal Museum.

The surrounding peat moors have been commercially excavated for many years and when the peat is worked out the area will be restored to the state it was in the distant past before the monks took a hand in 'improving' the land to enhance the finances of the abbey.

The Somerset Levels Project has been excavating in the area for some years. There are extensive displays in the County Museum at Taunton as well as in a small museum at the Peat Moors Visitor Centre just south of Wedmore on the minor road to Shapwick. Peat cutting tools and some early photographs along with artifacts, diagrams and photographs of the excavations make up the displays. The main feature of the excavations are the ancient tracks that have existed from prehistoric times. The most recent excavation is of the Sweet Track, dated to 3,200BC and thought to be the oldest road in the world.

Just to the south of Glastonbury lies **Street**, rather overshadowed by being so close by. It is nevertheless quite ancient, getting its name from the nearby Roman road or street. Two local families, the Clarks and the Moorlands, were mainly responsible for the present prosperity of the town. The Moorlands dealt in sheep skins, which they still do, and scoured the countryside for supplies. Clark's shoe factory has a very interesting museum. There may be seen displays of shoes dating from Roman times to the present day, and not just shoes but fashion plates, shoe buckles and shoe making machinery of the nineteenth century. Early advertising posters and a shoe snuff-box collection make up a remarkable and unusual museum very well worth the visit.

Additional Information

Accommodation

£ = expensive
££ = moderate
£££ = inexpensive
EM = evening meal available

Castle Cary

George Hotel (££, EM)
Market Place, BA7 7AH
☎ 01963 350761

Mrs C. Orland (£)
South Court, South Street, BA7 7ET
☎ 01963 351440
Food at the George Hotel.

Glastonbury

Number Three Restaurant & Hotel
   (£££, EM)
3 Magdalene Street, BA6 9EW
☎ 01458 832129

The Who'd A Thought It Inn (££, EM)
17 Northload Street, BA6 9JJ
☎ 01458 834460

Meadow Barn (£, EM)
Middlewick Farm,
Wick, BA6 8JW
☎ 01458 832351

Places to Visit

Castle Cary

Castle Cary Museum
Open: April-October 10am-12noon
and 2-4.30pm.

Hadspen House
☎ 01749 813707
Open: all year 9am-6pm.
Nursery open April-October except
Monday.

Glastonbury

Glastonbury Abbey
Ruins open daily all year.

Lake Village Museum
☎ 01458 832984 for details

Somerset Rural Life Museum
Abbey Farm, Chilkwell St, BA6 8DB
☎ 01458 831197
Open: April-October Monday-
Friday 10am-5pm, Saturday-
Sunday 2-6pm; November-March
Monday-Friday 10am-5pm,
Saturday 11am-4pm.

*Peat Moors Visitor Centre
    & Iron Age Farm*
Willows Garden Centre, Shapwick
Road, Westhay, Meare, BA6 9TT.
☎ 014586 257
Open: daily March-Sptember 9am-
6pm, November-February 9am-5pm.
Closed 25-26 December, 1 January.

Highbridge

The Levels Farm Visitor Centre
New Road Farm, East Huntspill,
near Burnham-on-Sea TA9 3PZ
☎ 01278 783250
Open: 10am-6pm Easter-September
daily, October-Easter Sunday only.

Ilchester

Fleet Air Arm Museum
Royal Naval Air Station,
Yeovilton BA22 8HT
☎ 01935 840565

Open: daily, except 24-25 December, from 10am weekdays and
Bank Holidays, 12.30pm Sunday;
closes 5.30pm or dusk if earlier.

Lyte's Cary Manor (NT)
Open: April-October, Monday,
Wednesday & Saturday 2-6pm, or
dusk if earlier.

Langport

Aller Moor Pumping Station
Burrow Bridge
Open: Monday to Friday all year.

Midelney Manor
Drayton
☎ 01458 251229
Open: May-September, Thursday
and Bank Holidays 2.30-5.30pm.

Muchelney Abbey
☎ 01458 250664
Open: April-September daily
10am-6pm.

Somerset Cider Brandy Company
Kingsbury Episcopi
☎ 01460 240782

Somerton

Stembridge Windmill (NT)
High Ham, TA10 9DJ
☎ 01458 250818
Open: April-September, Sunday,
Monday and Wednesday 2-5pm.

Stoke St Gregory

Willows & Wetlands Visitor Centre
Meare Green Court
☎ 0823 490249
Open: Monday-Friday, 9am-1pm,
2-5pm, Saturday 10am-1pm, 2-5pm.
Closed 25-26 December, 1 January.

Street

Clark's Shoe Museum
☎ 01458 431131
Open: Monday-Friday 10am-
4.45pm, Saturday 10am-5pm,
Sunday 11am-5pm.

Westonzoyland
Westonzoyland Pumping Station
Open: Bank Holiday Sunday and
Monday, and the first Sunday in
the month April-September.

Tourist Information Centres

Glastonbury
The Tribunal, 9 High Street
☎ 01458 832954

Wincanton
☎ 01963 34063

Glastonbury Abbey

Taunton & the Quantocks

3

On the A30 near the borders with Devon and Dorset is the small town of **Chard**. The town has Saxon origins and has been a borough since the thirteenth century. Almost the oldest building is the parish church, for in 1577 most of the town was burnt to the ground. Fore Street gives Chard a special character with a few of the buildings dating from the years just after the fire. The town hall, which is a focal point, is a Georgian building with a cupola, similar to the one at Bridport in Dorset.

Old Town has narrow streets and abrupt corners to explore. The grammar school was founded in 1671, though the building is older. Charles I passed by during the Civil War and bivouacked twice but there was no fighting. Judge Jeffreys hanged twelve Chard men following the Monmouth Rebellion. In the High Street is a plaque commemorating the inventor John Stringfellow, who made an aeroplane in 1847 and exhibited it at Crystal Palace in 1868. His models can be seen in the Science Museum in London. The trouble was that petrol, or aviation spirit, had not been refined so his engine relied on methylated spirit and John Stringfellow died without recognition.

At the heyday of the canals it was possible to take boats from Chard to Bridgwater. There is a museum in the town with exhibits showing local and industrial history.

Just to the north of the town, off the A358, is Hornsbury Mill. This nineteenth-century mill has been restored to working order, and there is a unique collection of bric-a-brac housed on the four floors of the mill building. The small grounds are attractive and there are ducks to feed on the mill pond. Chard offers trout fishing on the River Axe, as well as coarse fishing.

East towards Crewkerne the A30 climbs upward towards Windwhistle Hill. Here is a nine-hole golf course, and on the opposite side of the road is the village of **Cricket St Thomas**. The manor house was once the home of the Hood family; Admiral Hood was the most celebrated member of the family, his fame arising from his naval victories against the French in the eighteenth century.

Cricket St Thomas Wildlife Park was opened in 1967. There is an aviary, and 16 acres of gardens in addition to a 'TV theme park'. The Butterfly Breeding Unit allows the worldwide collection of butterflies to live in natural surroundings, and the Country Life Museum has a collection giving an insight into obsolete crafts. A working dairy farm is on display and milking can be seen. The heavy horse centre is a thrilling sight as these magnificent animals help with the daily farm work or run free in the fields. As with many old manor houses the church is close by; there are many interesting features in this, one of the smallest churches in the country.

Three miles north of Cricket St Thomas is the village of **Dowlish Wake**. Here the cider mills of Perry Brothers can be visited in a unique sixteenth-century barn, where there is a museum of farm bygones.

Four miles south-east of Chard is **Forde Abbey**, set in the lovely valley of the River Axe. The building was started early in the twelfth century but it was not finally completed until the fifteenth century. It was a flourishing Cistercian monastery and the history of its rise to riches and noble learning makes fascinating reading. Abbot Chard added to the building between 1500 and 1536. At the Dissolution of the monasteries, he gave the property to the king to save it from destruction. Much of the early building can still be seen including the refectory, dormitory and chapter house, which is now a chapel.

previous page: The gardens at Barrington Court

The house, last altered in 1650, contains a rich collection of furniture, pictures and tapestries. There are 30 acres of gardens, lakes and parkland, much of it the result of centuries of landscaping and planting. Forde Abbey Fruit Gardens offer the opportunity to pick strawberries, raspberries and currants in season, with the spectacular countryside as a backdrop.

Ilminster is about 6 miles northward from Chard. Ilminster means a minster on the River Isle. The fifteenth-century parish church of St Mary is of splendid proportions and the tower is thought to have been modelled on Wells Cathedral. A plaque on the George Hotel commemorates the visit of Queen Victoria — though she was only a baby at the time. The old grammar school was founded in 1586. There was once a flourishing lace-making industry in the town, and flax as well. The Saturday market has been flourishing for many years. Judge Jeffreys took a terrible retribution on the local Speke family, whose elder son led a troop in Monmouth's army. The elder son escaped abroad, but Judge Jeffreys hanged the younger son instead from a tree in the market place.

A walk from Ilminster starts near the Minster Church, where a lane runs south, soon swinging west. Go to the end then over the fields to Coldharbour, cross the river and turn right, downstream. Cross the river back and back again before crossing the main road to continue downstream. At the next footbridge cross the river again and go south-east back to the town.

Westport, a few miles north, was created as an inland port by the Parrett Navigation Company at the height of the canal era. Goods of many kinds, including cider, wool, stone and willows went out, with coal and machinery coming in.

One mile south of Westport is **Barrington** village and Barrington Court (National Trust). The house was built by Lord Daubeny in 1520 in the local Ham stone, and little external alteration has been made since. It has twisted finials and late Gothic windows. The seventeenth-century coach house and stables have been converted to a private dwelling. There are walled gardens, a restoration exhibition, a picnic area and a children's play area.

Barrington Court Estate has developed an Estate Trail. This offers the opportunity to see the management of an estate on an everyday basis. Over the past 70 years the estate has been developed with a caring approach to the environment and the trail has been developed as an educational facility, with a useful leaflet.

A pleasant drive through the lanes eastward for 3 miles leads to

Forde Abbey

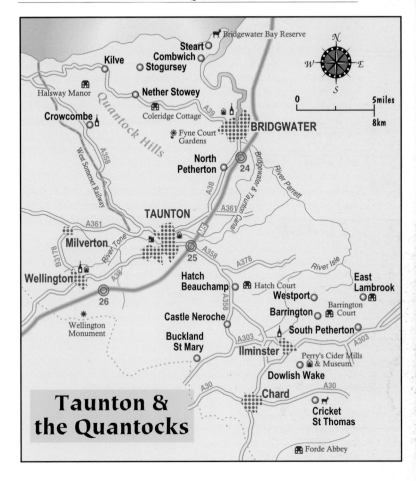

Taunton &
the Quantocks

East Lambrook with its manor, nursery and fish garden. The manor
is a fifteenth-century house, again built of local Ham stone. It is
furnished with period furniture throughout. The house is only open
in summer on Thursdays, but the gardens are open daily all year;
they and the nursery are laid out as an Elizabethan cottage garden.

Almost 6 miles due west of Ilminster is **Castle Neroche** and
Neroche Forest. This was once one of the great Somerset 'forests',
that is a hunting ground, not just an area covered with trees , and

Neroche Forest once covered five thousand acres. The castle was a prehistoric site. It was used by the Saxons just before the Norman invasion, then it was taken over by Count Robert of Mortain, a half brother to William the Conqueror. He built a timber tower and surrounded it by a timber palisade and deep ditches. Only 20 years later the site was abandoned in favour of Montacute, some 20 miles to the east. The forest is still over two thousand acres and is under the care of the Forestry Commission, who have laid out an attractive nature trail, and there is a picnic site in the forest park. The walk is 2½ miles long through mixed woodland with many streams, and with a short-cut back to the start for a walk of 1½ miles.

Castle Neroche is the eastern outpost of the Blackdown Hills. Priors Park picnic place is just to the west of the B3170 near Widcome. The setting is a former parkland set high on the hills, yet reasonably level and with an open grassy play area surrounded by oak, beech and larch.

East of Widcombe a road runs along the top of the hills, which in places marks the county boundary between Somerset and Devon to the south. To the north is the Vale of Taunton Deane. Near the western end of the hill is the Wellington Monument, an imposing obelisk built in 1818 to commemorate the exploits of the Duke of Wellington. The National Trust owns the long strip of land from the road to the obelisk, an area of just over 12 acres.

Past the monument and the crossroads, where the road turns sharply to the north, a small lane leads ahead. This bridleway, later unfenced, makes a fine walk over Blackdown Common with splendid views all round. It is just over the border in Devon.

Any of the minor roads at the western end of Blackdown Hill go north, down off the hills, crossing the M5 motorway, and into **Wellington**, which is under 3 miles from the monument. Wellington lies on the A38, once described as 'the longest lane in Britain', but fortunately the town has been saved from being throttled to death with traffic by the building of the M5 motorway. Between two and three hundred years ago weaving was being organised into an integrated industry from the scattered cottage industry that it was at that time. As in other parts of the west country, serge was the main product, with much of the cloth produced going to the Continent. A Wellington family of Quakers were the instigators of the integration of the weaving trade, and ran the ensuing firm for a hundred years. Then the business passed to the Fox family. As much of the business of the firm was on the Continent, members of both families spent a lot of time abroad learning the languages, and the firm's records contain many letters referring to the fact that business was conducted, if need be, in French, Dutch or German.

Light engineering and shopping came to the aid of the town as the weaving trade declined. Wellington has wide streets on each side of its central crossroads with a few Georgian houses. The classical town hall dominates the centre while the old church is at the eastern end. In the Perpendicular-style church is a stately tomb with a Corinthian pillared canopy. Here is buried Sir John Popham, the Lord Chief Justice when he died in 1607, who was the presiding judge at the trial of Guy Fawkes.

Wellington has a sports centre which has a 25m (82ft) heated indoor pool, a multiple sports hall, squash, sauna, and a dry ski slope.

Some 6 miles north-east along the A38 is the Somerset county town of **Taunton**, also accessible from junction 25 off the M5 motorway, and giving its name to the lovely Vale of Taunton Deane.

Taunton has always been at the centre of history in the area, no doubt because of the position the town occupies in the centre of the valley, with a river to make it more accessible. King Ine of Wessex fortified Taunton in AD710. Twelve years later according to the *Anglo-Saxon Chronicle* 'Queen Ethelburga razed Taunton'.

During medieval times Taunton flourished under the tolerant rule of the Bishops of Winchester. The fact that Taunton belonged to Winchester led to the town having a somewhat odd position through the years. The large ecclesiastical houses of Glastonbury and Wells owned much of Somerset and that led to smaller places than Taunton being developed as county towns. Ilchester, though much smaller, was county town for a while, as was Somerton.

Taunton Castle was built during the twelfth century when Henry of Blois was both Abbot of Glastonbury and Bishop of Winchester. He built a massive Norman keep which has now disappeared. Parts of the castle, especially the later additions, now house the county museum with natural history and archaeological exhibits and a fine Roman mosaic. A visual history of the county is given in the Somerset Light Infantry Museum. There are paintings and a collection of extinct mammals from the Mendip caves.

The castle grounds are also the venue for Shakespearian productions. The Great Hall of the castle was the scene of Judge Jeffreys's Bloody Assize, when as presiding judge he sent 150 people to their deaths, and many more to transportation. His ghost is said to walk on September nights — the month of the trials.

After these stirring times Taunton picked up the threads of its

Barrington Court

interrupted trade as a clothing centre. Serge making was predominant, later silk took over and the town became famous for its shirts and collars.

Since Stuart times rebuilding has occurred with most of the town architecture being Georgian or Victorian. The town centre now contains many modern buildings. Taunton is still a busy market town with an excellent shopping centre.

A pleasant walk, from near the railway station, is along the canal and back along the river bank. It is possible to make this walk 3 miles long by using the A38 for a quarter of a mile south from the canal to the river. By walking to Creech St Michael the distance would be 6 miles. The energetic could continue to Charlton, across the fields south to the river, and then back to the town, for a walk of 10 miles.

Also in Taunton and not to be missed are the Tudor House in Fore

Street and the seventeenth-century almshouses. Among the modern attractions are two eighteen-hole golf courses, bowls and tennis, fishing and an indoor swimming pool. There is a cinema and theatre, the Brewhouse Theatre and Art Centre. From behind the castle an attractive walk follows the banks of the River Tone, while in Vivary Park beyond the High Street there are pleasant gardens with a jogging trail, a model railway and a model boating pond.

Near the Somerset County Cricket Club's ground the Priory Barn has been restored as the Somerset Cricket Museum. The building, which dates from the late fifteenth and early sixteenth centuries, is thought to have been a gate house or lodgings house for the priory, the location of which is not precisely known.

Trull is 1½ miles south of Taunton on a minor road. The church, which dates from the thirteenth century, has some of the best examples of wood carving in the area and is worth a visit.

The area round Taunton is fruit country with its fertile land that made Taunton and Norton Fitzwarren famous names in the world of cider. Cider is still made at Norton Fitzwarren by the Taunton Cider Company. Farmhouse cider has been made since cider makers came with the invading Norman armies. The craft of cider

Cycling on the Quantocks

making became concentrated in larger establishments as the drink's popularity grew and the smaller farmhouse producers have mostly gone out of business. Just over 4 miles west from Taunton on the A38 is the establishment of R. J. Sheppy and Son, makers of farmhouse cider. Visitors can see the vat store and press room of a small traditional cider works. Over 40 acres of orchards may be viewed along with a small farm and the cider museum.

About 4 miles south of Taunton on the A358 road towards Ilminster is the village of **Hatch Beauchamp**. To the west, down narrow lanes, is the RSPCA animal centre and wildlife field unit (signposted off the main road). As well as stray dogs and cats it is possible to find anything in temporary residence from a dormouse to a deer. The aim of the centre is eventually to return wild creatures to the wild after they have been restored to health. A small exhibition of pictures dealing with the work of the National Oiled Seabird Cleaning Centre, which is also housed here, is worth a visit.

Across the main road is **Hatch Court**, a fine mansion in the Palladian style and built of Bath stone, with its nearby medieval church of St John the Baptist. In the house there is a magnificent stone staircase, seventeenth- and eighteenth-century furniture, paintings, a china room and a small Canadian Military Museum.

North of Taunton rises the massif of the Quantock Hills, with the highest point at 358m (1,200ft). On the eastern side the slopes are gentle as the central plateau gives way to rolling hills. To the west the slopes are much steeper and the whole area is famous for the wooded combes which cut into the hills on all sides.

A well known walk along the Quantock crest is one of the joys of the area and is a favourite walk for ramblers. It is almost 9 miles long and gives fantastic views on all sides. The main A39 Bridgwater to Minehead road squeezes round between the northern end of the hills and the sea. Along here are car parking spaces and tracks leading up to Pardlestone Hill, Longstone Hill and Beacon Hill. It is quite a steep climb so take it gently with plenty of time to look at the views.

The picnic site provided by the Forestry Commission as part of their forest park recreation scheme can be approached from the A39 at Nether Stowey, from where it is signposted. Situated in Rams Combe it is a very pleasant streamside site in a valley bottom surrounded by conifers and mature Douglas fir. Starting at the picnic site is the Quantock Forest Trail, a 3-mile walk with forest views that climbs through mixed woodland and the remnants of an old oak coppice. It crosses a stream and climbs to a fine viewpoint.

There is varied bird life in the forest including red deer.

Also at **Nether Stowey** is Coleridge Cottage, owned by the National Trust. Samuel Taylor Coleridge lived in the cottage from 1796 to 1799, and it was here he wrote *The Ancient Mariner*. Only the parlour is open some summer afternoons. There are no facilities at the cottage, but meals and teas are available in the village.

Two miles away towards the coast is the village of **Stogursey**. Although it is a quiet place now, back in the twelfth century the local lord, called Fulke de Breaute, gathered in his castle a band of robbers who terrorised the surrounding countryside before he was brought to justice. The remains of the castle can still be seen. From Stogursey there is a walk over the fields, or down the lanes if the going is muddy, to Wick and then to Stolford on the coast. A left turn along the footpath gives a good close view of Hinkley Point nuclear power station. On this featureless stretch of coast the mighty strength of the square buildings match the long horizontal lines of the coast. These coastal paths were made many years ago when the coastguards made regular patrols. From here the coast path goes right along to East Quantoxhead about 7 miles away, or it is possible to cut back from the power station or the villages of Burton or Lilstock. One can turn back up to the village of **Kilve** and have a look at the church and the remains of the chantry. If you approach by car from the main road there is a good beach down the track beyond the church.

On the other side of the hills quietly tucked away on a minor road is the village of **Crowcombe**, the gem of all the Quantock villages, comfortably nestling against the south-western face of the hills. Crowcombe is dominated by the eighteenth-century brick and Ham stone mansion of Crowcombe Court. The church, like so many in the county, has some bench ends which are splendid, even by Somerset's high standards. The carvings include a mermaid and two men spearing a dragon. The church, mostly Perpendicular of a high standard, has a fine south aisle and a fan-vaulted southern porch.

Not far away, north-eastward, is the hamlet of **Halsway** and Halsway Manor, a historic house with some fine decorated ceilings and panelling. It is open throughout the year, unless it is being used for a conference (it is now a folk music and dance centre) so check locally before visiting.

North-east of the Quantock Hills is **Bridgwater**, which derives its name from the Norman knight Burgh Walter, who was given the estate following the Conquest. A castle was built to guard what was probably the best crossing of the Parrett estuary if the traveller

Coleridge Cottage, Nether Stowey

wished to avoid the worst of the mud. As the Danes were retreating from a defeat by the Saxons under King Alfred it was probably to Bridgwater that they came. This was in the ninth century and the place was fortified at that time. In the Civil War Lord Goring surrendered at Bridgwater in 1645 to Cromwell after a defeat at Langport by Cromwell's New Army. The Norman castle was demolished after the restoration. St Mary's Church, dating from the fourteenth century, is the town's sole remaining medieval building. It was from this church tower that James, Duke of Monmouth, saw the Royalist army approaching and planned the unsuccessful surprise attack which led to the Battle of Sedgemoor in 1685. The church has a graceful tall spire and among its many features are a Jacobean screen in a side chapel and a painting of the *Descent from the Cross*, attributed to an unknown Italian artist.

A Georgian area survives from the days when Bridgwater planned to rival Bristol as a port. The best houses are in Castle Street between King Street and the quay. Taunton was linked by canal and Bridgwater was the main port of entry for much of central and west Somerset, with boat traffic going many miles up the rivers feeding into the Parrett. The old docks with their warehouses can be seen in this historic port, which saw the Bristol Channel paddle steamers plying regularly to South Wales and Burnham-on-Sea.

Outside the market hall is a statue to Admiral Blake, a son of the town born in 1599. He won fame as a soldier defending Taunton during a year-long siege. Later he became Admiral of The Fleet to Cromwell, a position he held for 9 years; he is rated second only to Lord Nelson. The Blake museum has much material relating to his career, with other displays on the history of the town and district with archaeology and the Battle of Sedgemoor being featured. The friary, the town hall and hospital of St John are also worth noting.

Downstream is the village of **Combwich**, possibly an unloading place for the larger ships not risking coming further upstream. This was the last ford across the river and large numbers of skeletons have been unearthed at various times below the old ford indicating a large battle. A favourite topic of controversy for antiquarians is whether this was *Kynuit*, the site of a Saxon victory over the Danes.

Beyond Combwich is **Steart**, a hamlet almost in the Bristol Channel. Steart has a bird sanctuary and nature reserve. The tides race in at a phenominal rate over two miles offshore, so make sure you keep your feet dry. A footpath goes from Castle Field in Bridgwater along the riverbank down to Steart, making a 12 mile walk. Short cuts back can be made through the village of Chilton Trinity.

Just outside Bridgwater, on a minor road south of the A39, is the village of **Durleigh** and the nearby reservoir offers trout fishing. A little over a mile beyond and just before the village of **Enmore**, is a nine-hole golf course. Beyond the village the next turning right, north, towards Four Forks leads to **Barford Park**. Barford House is a small Queen Anne mansion in stone and red brick set in a large garden. The rooms with contemporary furniture are in daily family use. There is a walled flower garden, woodland and water gardens, and an archery glade.

Two and half miles south is the hamlet of **Broomfield** and Fyne Court Gardens (National Trust). These are the pleasure grounds that were attached to the house, which was demolished following a disastrous fire in 1898. The remnants of the building, the library and the music room are still in use, the latter being used for lectures and social events. The Somerset Trust for Nature Conservation has its headquarters here and the grounds are a nature reserve. There are pleasant woodland walks, a nature trail, lake, walled garden, two ponds and a small arboretum.

Additional Information

Accommodation

£££ = expensive
££ = moderate
£ = inexpensive
EM = evening meal available

Bridgwater

Friarn Court Hotel (££, EM)
37 St Mary Street, TA6 3LX
☎ 01278 452859

Quantock View House (£, EM)
Bridgwater Road
North Petherton TA6 6PR
☎ 01278 663309

Chard

Lordleaze Hotel (£, EM)
Lordleaze Lane, off Forton Road,
TA20 2HW
☎ 01460 61066

Ilminster

Hornsbury Mill Hotel (££, EM)
Eleighwater, TA20 2AQ
☎ 01460 63317

Nether Stowey

Mrs Lilienthal (£, EM)
Parsonage Farm, Over Stowey,
TA5 1HA
☎ 01278 733237

Taunton

Castle Hotel (£££, EM)
Castle Green, TA1 1NF
☎ 01823 272671

Farthings Hotel & Restaurant (£££, EM)
Hatch Beauchamp, TA3 6SG

The Jays Nest Country Hotel (££, EM)
Meare Green, Stoke St Gregory,
TA3 6HZ
☎ 01823 490250

Orchard House (££, EM)
Fons George, Wilton, TA1 3JS
☎ 01823 351783

Places to Visit

Bridgwater

Admiral Blake Museum
Blake Street
☎ 01278 456127
Open: Monday-Saturday 11am-
5pm, Sunday 2-5pm.

Barford Park
Spaxton
☎ 01278 671269
Open by appointment only.

Fyne Court (NT)
Broomfield
Open: all year daily 9am-6pm or
sunset if earlier.

Chard

Chard Museum
Open: May-September Monday-
Saturday.

Cricket St Thomas Wildlife Park
☎ 01460 30755
Open: summer 10am-6pm, winter
10am to dusk.

Forde Abbey & Gardens
☎ 01460 220231
House open: April-October,
Sunday, Wednesday & Bank
Holidays 1-4.30pm.
Garden open: daily 10am-4.30pm.

Hornsbury Mill
Open: daily 10.30am-6pm, Sunday
2-7pm.

Ilminster

Barrington Court (NT)
☎ 01460 41480.
Garden open: April-September
Saturday-Thursday, 11am-5.30pm.
Court house open: early April to
late September, Wednesday 11am-
5pm.

Perry's Cider Mills
Dowlish Wake
Open: Monday-Friday 9am-1pm,
1.30-5.30pm; Saturday and Bank
Holidays 9.30am-1pm, 1.30-
4.30pm; Sunday10am-1pm.

Nether Stowey
Coleridge's Cottage (NT)
Parlour only open: April-September, Tuesday, Wednesday &
Sunday 2-5pm.

South Petherton
East Lambrook Manor
☎ 01460 240328
Open: March-October Monday-
Saturday and Bank Holidays 10am-
5pm.

Taunton
Hatch Court
Hatch Beauchamp, TA3 6AA
☎ 0182 480120
Open: mid-June to mid-September
Thursday (house & garden),
Tuesday & Wednesday (garden
only) 2.30-5.30pm (last tour 5pm).

RSPCA West Hatch Wildlife Hospital
West Hatch
☎ 01823 480156
Visitor centre open: daily 9am-
4.30pm. Liable to change as birds &
animals are restored to the wild.

Sheppy's Cider & Rural Life Museum
Three Bridges, Bradford-on-Tone
☎ 01823 461233

Open: Monday-Saturday May-
September 8.30am-6.30pm,
October-April 8.30-6pm. Sunday
(Easter to Christmas) 12noon-2pm.

Somerset County Museum
& Somerset Light Infantry Museum
Castle Green
☎ 01823 255504
Open: Monday-Saturday 10am-5pm.

Somerset Cricket Museum
Priory Bridge Road, TA1 1XX
☎ 01823 275893
Open: March-October, Monday-
Saturday 10am-4pm.

Wellington
Wellington Museum
☎ 1749 673477
Open: Easter-October Monday-
Saturday 10am-4pm.

Tourist Information Centres
Bridgwater (open summer only)
50 High Street
☎ 01278 427652 or 424391 ext 419

Chard
The Guildhall, Fore Street
☎ 01460 67463

Ilminster
☎ 01460 57294

Taunton
The Library, Corporation Street
☎ 01823 274785

Wellington
The Squirrel, Fore Street
☎ 01823 474747

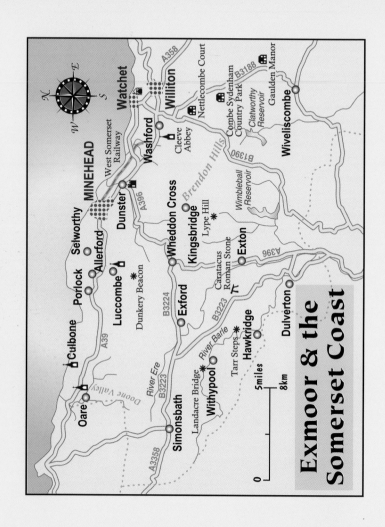

Exmoor & the Somerset Coast

opposite: Exmoor near Dunkery Beacon

Exmoor & the Somerset Coast

North-west Somerset includes Exmoor, with some of its 689sq km (265sq miles) in Devon but just over 70 per cent in Somerset. The highest point is Dunkery Beacon at 443m (1,705ft). There are many fine walks in the area: high ridges on the moors or sheltered valleys following fast flowing streams.

On the coastal strip there is the Somerset and North Devon Coast Path, now extended into the South West Peninsula Path which runs all the way round the coast to Bournemouth. The section in Somerset runs from the county line to Minehead and offers fine sea views. There are many short walks and nature trails in the area, a visit to one of the five information offices (some run by the National Trust and some by the National Park) will provide leaflets to all the walks.

At County Gate on the A39, there is a car park and an information office open in the summer. Just over the border and on the seaward side of the road is Old Barrow, or Burrow, one of the few Roman remains on Exmoor. Raiding across the channel from South Wales was a threat the Romans seem to have taken seriously. This small fort was garrisoned by about eighty legionaries under command of a centurion. From the car park at County Gate a hut circle and a viewpoint are not far away towards Lynton.

Badgworthy Water forms the boundary between Somerset and Devon. This is Lorna Doone country, made famous by R. D. Blackmore's novel. East from County Gate the first turning right leads down to **Oare** church, which was the scene of Lorna Doone's interrupted wedding. Inside the church is a memorial to the author. At the tiny hamlet of **Malmesmead**, turn right at the church where there is a picnic site and a gift shop. A pony trekking stable completes this tiny hamlet. By going upstream the Doone Valley can be reached, the lower part of Hoccombe Combe, just before Badgworthy Hill. One may walk up the road to reach a public footpath, to the Doone Valley, which rejoins the river higher up. Or pay the local farmer a modest fee to follow the river all the way, for a 4-mile round trip.

Did the Doones exist, were they fact or legend? Well, the Doones did exist and Jon Ridd went to school at Tiverton, but Blackmore's masterpiece is a work of fiction. However there *was* much lawlessness and feuding in many country areas and the wilds of Exmoor remained that way longer than most due to the difficulty of access to that area. Possibly adding fuel to the flames was the action of one landowner in bringing in Scottish families, dispossessed during the Highland clearances. These migrants, one can imagine, may not have got on very well with the locals. The landowner hoped the hardy northerners would more easily come to terms with the wild country and help tame it.

The rivers that run north from Exmoor, the East Lyn, Farley Water, Hoaroak Water and Badgworthy Water are fed by many tributaries. To the north the moor is steep and in times of heavy rain these rivers can rise very swiftly. Northward from The Chains, which lie west from Brendon Two Gates, are many small streams fed by the marshy area below the ridge. From the official annual rainfall figures: Minehead 35in (89cm), Dulverton 60in (152cm) and The Chains 80in (203cm), it is obvious that the area up on the moors can be quite damp. In normal times the peat soaks up the rain to release it gradually, draining into the streams. However if rain is heavy and continuous then flooding in the lower reaches occurs as the peat on the moors can absorb no more water, and the rain runs straight off. The water from the majority of the northern watershed runs down through Lynton and Lynmouth. Such conditions caused the disaster of 1952 when floods almost destroyed Lynmouth.

All this is the harsh wintry side of the moor, far removed from the mood which caused R. D. Blackmore to write 'the land lies softly'. From the car park area on the B3223 near Brendon Common a signposted footpath leads to the Doone Valley and over the moor, for a walk of about 4 miles there and back.

The smooth hills of central Exmoor near **Simonsbath** are coated with blue moor grass or tawny deer sedge. The valleys may be bare and smooth, marshy or tree covered. Often the headwaters of the rivers run from peaty channels, many stained with iron ore. The mood of the streams is different in the valleys where the peat channels become trout streams.

In spring the wooded valleys wear carpets of bluebells surrounded by banks where the earlier primroses grow. At all times of the year grey-green lichen can be found on the rocks and trees. The Exe and the Barle, on the southern side of the watershed, are gentler rivers as they wind through wooded valleys on their way to the south coast. Along the coast and the heather moors can be found miniature forests of cotton grass. Pink orchids and red lichens form brighter patches against the gentler colours of sphagnum moss and sundews found round the marshy areas.

To many visitors one of the greatest charms of Exmoor is its variety, which has an influence on the wildlife of the area. Exmoor ponies are often seen. They are not wild, in the sense that they do not belong to anyone, and their interests are looked after by the Exmoor Pony Society. Much more difficult to spot are the wild red deer. It is believed that between 800 and 1,000 belong to this, the largest herd of red deer in England, and their territory takes in the Quantock Hills. One of the earliest packs of staghounds is believed to have been kept by Hugh Pollard in 1598, and there is little doubt that regular hunting has taken place since the middle of the seventeenth century.

There are many foxes and rabbits, and badgers are common, though they prefer the lower areas to the open moor. Grey squirrels appear all over the area and other residents include stoats, weasels, hedgehogs, hares and moles. As for bird life a better reserve could not have been built, the list seems impossibly long, as the great variety of landscape — open moor, woodland, streams and coast — provide such an abundance of habitat in a relatively small area. Dipper and grey wagtail can be seen along the fast flowing streams. Along the Barle kingfishers and moorhens nest. In many of the waters herons fish, and there is a heronry at Coppleham Cross near Winsford. There are sandpipers and sand martins, chats, warblers and finches. Open moorland makes up just over 25 per cent of the whole National Park. Relatively small numbers of both red and black grouse survive on the moor. While snipe, curlew and lapwing are regular nesters, the meadow pipit and skylark are the most common. Whinchat and wheatear, and the ring ousel are summer visitors, a few merlin nest on the moor. Rarer species like the hen harrier, rough legged buzzard, great grey shrike and snow bunting have all been spotted occasionally. In addition all the small birds associated with the English countryside may be found, the robin, wren and blackbird, chaffinch, greenfinch and all the tit family to name but a few.

History can be seen on all sides round the moor and in the villages and towns. There are Bronze Age barrows such as Alderman's ⛰ Barrow north of Exford or Chapman's Barrow, as well as earthworks such as Cow Castle and Mounsey both beside the River Barle. Cow Castle can be reached by a 2-mile riverside bridleway south from Simonsbath. From **Hawkridge** church a road used as a public path follows Hawkridge ridge in a south-easterly direction to dive down to the river where there is a footbridge crossing to Mounsey ❋ Castle. North of the village of Hawkridge is Tarr Steps, but do not be confused by the map, as there is no road bridge and the car park is

Tarr Steps clapper bridge

The ford at Winsford

on the northern side. Tarr Steps is a fine example of a clapper bridge, with large flat stones placed across the tops of upright stones. These clapper bridges date from the medieval times, so they have obviously stood the test of time. Approach from Winsford and cross the B3223 at Spire Cross. There is plenty of parking space and Tarr Steps Farm has morning coffee, lunch and cream teas.

Close by **Spire Cross** is the Caractacus Stone left mysteriously by the Romans. Caractacus was a Celtic chief whom the Romans defeated and took prisoner. They were, however, so impressed by his noble bearing that they did not kill him, the usual fate of chiefs during Roman invasions. The inscription on the stone is translated as 'a descendant of Caractacus'. Caractacus was a common Celtic name, but the stone is a genuine relic of the fifth or sixth century AD. It lies just within the boundary of a piece of National Trust land that encompasses the top of Winsford Hill; a mile north-west along the main road is the summit, at 426m (1,397ft), a viewpoint and the Wambarrows.

More recent are the packhorse bridges at Dunster and Allerford, which is near Porlock. Most of the churches are medieval, as are many of the farm buildings. Exmoor has no relics of the Neolithic period to rival Stonehenge. There are however many stone circles, though they are not spectacular and have many stones missing. Solitary standing stones are numerous, though it is difficult to prove which are antiquities and which have been erected in more recent centuries as rubbing posts for cattle.

Exmoor was a royal forest and remained almost undisturbed until the 1800s. In the sixteenth century there were some 40,000 sheep on the moor, which is heavy usage even by today's standards. The Knight family were principally responsible for much of the moor as it appears today with its pattern of scattered farms and enclosures, which they created. In earlier times there were no roads on the moor and transport was by packhorse. John Knight constructed nearly 30 miles of new roads, and a similar length of boundary walls. He had his headquarters at Simonsbath which grew from an isolated farmhouse to a small village. The family introduced arable farming to the area round Simonsbath though grazing was predominant. John Knight's son, Sir Frederick, prospected for minerals. Little was found except for iron, and for a while there was an iron mine near the village and a railway was started, but never completed. The iron mines here were closed in 1860, they re-opened briefly early this century but finally closed in 1914.

There were iron mines on the Brendon Hills; in the mid-eighteenth century there were about fourteen mines in production. The ore went by railway to Watchet and on to South Wales and traces of the railway can still be found.

The villages of Exmoor hide in the valleys and sheltered combes, the white or grey stone houses often having their weather end to the west. In the villages are a variety of attractive churches and cosy inns. The churches have their own individual attractions, from the tiny church at Oare to the larger parish church of Porlock, which has a truncated spire, and Dunster which is a double conventual church.

Before leaving this area, try to visit Landacre Bridge, a fine local stone bridge in a moorland setting. From the car park just south of the bridge a footpath goes downstream to **Withypool**, a round trip of about 4 miles. Up through Withypool village is a cosy little pub for refreshments before walking back again.

The road descends from the moor to **Dulverton**. By the river bridge is Exmoor House and the Exmoor National Park information centre where maps, photographs and other items of interest are displayed and experienced staff are on hand to answer enquiries. Guided walks, organised by the Park authority and led by volunteer guides, are available on most days in the summer. Dulverton is a small country town bustling with farmers, tourists, huntsmen and fishermen. The town once had a Norman fort, Mounsey, or so it is said, but it seems remote from the present town. The remains of St Nicholas Priory are on top of the hill north-west of the town.

From Dulverton the A396 is a pleasant drive, northwards along the River Exe valley towards **Wheddon Cross**. This valley is the boundary between Exmoor and the Brendon Hills. For the last few miles the road follows the River Quarme, but north of Wheddon Cross it starts to follow the River Avill towards Dunster. At Wheddon Cross turn onto the B3224, but soon turn off up to Dunkery Gate and back to the moor. Just over 3 miles from the village is a car park and a viewpoint looking northwards to the coast. Leave the car and walk up the gentle rise to Exmoor's highest point, Dunkery Beacon. Dunkery is on National Trust land; in 1944 Sir Richard Acland, of a famous Exmoor family (an ancestor Sir Thomas Acland had been a warden of the forest) gave nearly 10,000 acres of his estate to the National Trust. This has been extended by other gifts and purchases into the Holnicote Estate of over 12,000 acres. The estate has nearly 7,000 acres of moorland and includes some of the loveliest parts of the area.

Just over 1½ miles due north, down a steep hill, is Cloutsham nature trail, a 3-mile walk over moorland and through oak woods.

Lower down is **Luccombe** with an unusual thatched church.

Dunster has a fine main street with the castle dominating one end, guarding the valley, and the seventeenth-century yarn market at the other end. During the Civil War the Royalists held the castle for 160 days against a siege by the Parliamentarians. This was the Royalists' last stronghold in Somerset as they retreated west. The castle, started by William de Mohun soon after the Norman invasion, was built on the site of a Saxon fort, and was remodelled in the nineteenth century. In 1376 the castle was bought by Lady Elizabeth Luttrell and it remained in the hands of the Luttrell family until, in 1975, the property was given to the National Trust.

Among the many features of the castle are the carved elm staircase and the elaborate seventeenth-century plaster ceiling in the dining room. There is a fine collection of English furniture and a unique set of sixteenth-century leather hangings is on show in the banqueting hall. Outdoors there are terraces of sub-tropical plants, with fine views of the Bristol Channel and the moors. There is a National Trust information office and a shop at the castle, and it is possible to picnic in the park.

Nearby is Dunster Castle mill, on the site of a mill mentioned in the Domesday Book. The present mill dates from the eighteenth

Dunster yarn market and castle

century. It was restored in 1979 and can be reached from Mill Lane, the car park, or the castle gardens. The yarn market, built by George Luttrell about 1600, is a covered market used for displaying the smooth 'kersey' cloth manufactured in the village. Look for a hole in a rafter made by a cannon shot during the Civil War siege.

The nearby Luttrell Arms is a medieval building and may have

Cleeve Abbey gatehouse

been the home, at one time, of the Abbot of Cleeve. The old dove-cote, probably dating from the twelfth century, still has the revolving ladder used to reach the nesting boxes. The church, which was formerly part of the priory, has the longest rood screen in England. Conygar Tower, on the nearby hill, is not a medieval building but is Georgian Gothick.

The Brendon Hills are included in the Exmoor National Park. However, little open moorland remains as this lower land has been fenced and improved for many generations. The result is high rolling fields and woodlands, the highest point being **Lype Hill**, at 423m (1,390ft). There is a picnic site not far from the summit from where it is possible to take a walk through the woods. A climb up the combe, leads out onto Lype Common and up to the summit. A detour can be made on the way back to make an almost circular walk.

Lype Hill is the highest point in Somerset after Exmoor itself and there are fine views from the top over the moors to the west. The nearby villages of Kingsbridge and Luxborough once provided accommodation for the miners on the Brendon Hills. Mining went on sporadically for many years; the mid-nineteenth century was the heyday, when a mining village grew up on Brendon Hill. It was virtually owned by the mine owners and as it was a temperance village, thirsty miners had to walk to Raleigh Cross to get a drink. There was even a railway down to Watchet to ship the iron ore across to South Wales. This line closed finally just about the time of World War I. The village had a mission church, two nonconformist chapels, a general shop and a warehouse. There was even a Temperance Hotel which no doubt was the headquarters of the Brendon Hill and Gupworthy Temperance Society and the Brendon Hill Teetotal Drum and Fife Band.

All the miners have gone now, but traces remain of the village and the railway, which had a very steep incline down its higher reach. Sea View House which once housed the mine 'captions' still stands, as does the Methodist chapel to the west of Raleigh Cross Inn. However, Beulah Terrace, a row of miners' houses, is in ruins. The great incline down to Comberow will probably never be obliterated from the landscape, such a large work will leave its traces probably for ever. A ruined winding house, once used to haul up the mine trucks, stands by the side of the incline.

The minor road via Roadwater continues on to Washford. Just before the main road is a car park serving **Cleeve Abbey.** This was a Cistercian abbey founded by the Earl of Lincoln towards the end of the twelfth century. Sufficient remains for the visitor to get a good impression of what a modestly sized abbey was like. Nowhere, not even at any of the other Cistercian houses, do the domestic buildings survive as well as at Cleeve. The combined gatehouse and almonry stands, the dormitory stairs and the monks' common room. A splendid wagon roof covers the hall, medieval wall paintings and a pavement with heraldic tiles are among the notable features. Possibly the main reason why the abbey is so well preserved is that it was held in high esteem by the local gentry. At the time of the Dissolution they put in an unsuccessful plea for the continuance of the house. The seventeen monks were found to be above average in the work they did for charity and had a good reputation for being honest and hardworking.

On the opposite side of the hills is **Wimbleball Lake**, the largest lake in the area. It is over 2 miles long, winding round the hills. It has been created by the South-West Water Authority as a reservoir by damming the River Haddon, and facilities for recreation are pro- vided. Set among some of the most beautiful scenery of Exmoor there are glorious views, woodland walks and a nature reserve. A picnic site is provided with plenty of space for children to play, set against the colourful spectacle of the sailing boats. The lake is kept stocked with fish for fly fishermen to test their skills. Approach from the A396 and Brompton Regis or the B3190 by way of Upton to Haddon Hill where there is a parking space for the viewpoint south towards Wellington and Tiverton. The National Park authority has an information office at the lake.

On the B3188 Watchet to Taunton road there are four places of interest to visit. Working southwards they are Nettlecombe Court (the ancestral home of the Raleigh and Trevelyan families from the sixteenth century, and now a field study centre), Combe Sydenham Hall, Combe Fisheries and Gaulden Manor.

Combe Sydenham Country Park, a private 500-acre estate rich in scenic beauty and steeped in history is open to the public. The Elizabethan manor, built in 1580, was the home of Elizabeth Syden- ham, the second wife of Sir Francis Drake. In the Courtroom of the West Wing can be seen Drake's legendary cannonball. Elizabeth, tired of waiting for Sir Francis to return from sea, was going to marry another. On her way to the wedding a meteorite struck the path in front of her and she took this as a sign to wait to marry Drake, which she did. The meteorite has since been known as Drake's cannonball. The medieval cornmill, mentioned in the Domesday Survey, has been restored and produces flour daily for a

Watchet Harbour

new craft bakery. There are woodland walks, fishponds and a deerpark to enjoy.

Sir George Sydenham fought on the side of the king in the Civil War, and his ghost is said to ride down Sydenham Combe on certain nights.

Combe Fisheries lie in the deep valley by Combe Sydenham Farm close to the hall and the ancient deer park. The ponds are fed by springs which in turn feed from the Brendon Hills. They were laid out about the time of the marriage of Sir Francis Drake to Elizabeth Sydenham, and are now a modern trout hatchery. Visitors can feed the fish and have the opportunity to purchase trout, either fresh or smoked on the premises.

On the very edge of Exmoor, where the valley begins to widen out into the Valley of Taunton Dene, is **Gaulden Manor**. It is 9 miles north-west of Taunton off the B3188 near Tolland. Built of local red sandstone the present house is fifteenth century, but the manor itself dates from the twelfth century. There are herb and bog gardens and plant sales. Guided tours are led by the owners. The house was once the home of the Turbervilles of Bere Regis.

Back on the coast there is still much to see and do. **Watchet** docks, once busy with iron ore, have recently been given a new lease of life. Many small coastal ports declined and silted up when railways took the coastal trade away. At one time almost all goods were carried by sailing boats, which managed to get a surprisingly long way inland. No doubt easier road access to the Midlands since the M5 was built has helped the trade for this small harbour.

The church at Watchet is dedicated to St Decuman, a Welsh saint from the Dark Ages. He is supposed to have come ashore from a raft, bringing a cow to provide him with milk. The church and dock is featured in Coleridge's *The Ancient Mariner*, for it was from here that the crew set sail. Watchet museum reflects the history of the port from Saxon days right up to the present day, including both maritime and mining connections.

In the mid-nineteenth century about 30,000 tons of iron ore from the Brendon Hills were being shipped each year. Watchet was an important port in Saxon days. In those violent times it was attacked and burnt by the Danes on at least three occasions. It is the family seat of the Windham family whose memorials can be seen in the church. The family played an important part in Somerset history. Colonel Francis Windham commanded the garrison of Dunster Castle during the siege of the Civil War. Nearby was the home of

The West Somerset Railway, near Watchet

Robert Fitzurse, one of the murderers of Thomas a' Becket. The restored West Somerset Railway passes through the town.

Just over the hill to the west is **Old Cleeve**. Here are the sheepskin workshops of John Wood and Son. During the summer months visitors are offered a guided tour of the works, seeing the process from the raw skin to the finished products, including rugs and slippers.

Blue Anchor has a useful expanse of sands — but is visibly marred by its caravan sites, while **Minehead** is a blend of old harbour town and modern seaside resort. The holiday camp is well concealed at one end of the town with the eighteen-hole golf course beyond that. At the other end of the town, sheltering beneath the towering North Hill, is the old harbour with its lifeboat station. North Hill is a high wooded extension of Exmoor. Just beyond the lifeboat station is the North Hill nature trail, 3 miles long.

The town has a firm sandy beach and an outdoor bathing pool. There is a theatre and boating, riding and fishing. Little England is a model of a typical English country town complete with model railway.

Minehead is one of the oldest towns in Somerset, and the name is probably of Celtic origin. In 1265 much damage was done in the town by a marauding band of Welshmen before they were defeated by troops from Dunster Castle. The church on North Hill is dedicated to St Michael and dates from the fifteenth century; its tower served for many years as a beacon for ships approaching the harbour. The harbour was thought to be one of the safest on the north coast and remained secure in the great hurricane of 1703 which wreaked havoc in many other places.

From the late nineteenth century up to very recent years the Bristol Channel Paddle Steamers brought in day trippers on outings from Bristol and Newport. The fantastic acceleration, stopping power, and manoeuvrability of the paddle boats made them very suitable for the Bristol Channel ports, especially the winding channel up the Avon to Bristol.

The heyday of Minehead's harbour was in the seventeenth century when coarse Irish wool was imported for the weavers of Taunton. The town arms show a woolpack and a ship, but when the Taunton clothiers fell on hard times so Minehead's shippers fell with them. There is a short history of shipbuilding round the harbour. The population fell from nearly two thousand to a little over one thousand during the eighteenth century. When the once prolific herring shoals left the Somerset coast, things became worse. The growth in popularity of visiting seaside resorts and romantic scenery came to the rescue and Minehead prospered with that cult.

The West Somerset Railway, which terminates in the town, is the longest privately owned railway in England. It was originally sanctioned by an Act of Parliament in 1857 and the line opened in 1862 and reached Minehead in 1874. In 1923 the company became part of the Great Western Railway. British Railways took over in 1948 until 1971 when the line was closed. The present company was formed in 1971 but it was not until 1975 that trains ran. To operate as a viable company it is necessary to use diesel as well as steam, but the steam trains operate during summer months as a tourist attraction.

The line has featured many times on films and television; the star locomotive *The Flockton Flyer* has had a complete refit. Highlight of the line's tourist attraction is the Pullman Service. In first class Pullman dining cars a full four-course lunch is served as a steam engine hauls the train through the wooded hills and dales of West Somerset.

A good long, leg-stretching, walk from Minehead is to take the Somerset and North Devon Coast Path from its start near the church in Higher Town. It climbs up over North Hill to visit Selworthy Beacon before dropping down to Bassington. Walk back to **Allerford**, to see the pack horse bridge and the picturesque cottages, and take the path to the picturesque village of **Selworthy** with its thatched cottages. There is a fine view to Dunkery Beacon from the church at the top of the village. There is also a National Trust information office and shop, during summer months. From here it is possible to climb back up the hill again and wend your way back to Minehead; a round trip of about 12 miles with fine sea views. Both Allerford and Selworthy are noted for their walnut trees.

Porlock, with its infamous hill so dreaded by early motorists, has an earlier claim to fame than Minehead. Porlock was attacked in AD918 by Danish pirates, but the attack was beaten off by the townspeople. In the year AD1052 the last English king, Harold, landed at Porlock, attacked the town and set it alight. He had been living in exile in Ireland at this time, and his comeback lasted only a few years until 1066. There is a car park near the end of the B3225 at Porlock Weir, where the quaint harbour can be found. Porlock has narrow, winding streets and thatched cottages. The parish church dates from the thirteenth century, and has the splendid tomb of Sir John Harrington, who died in 1418.

The ascent of Porlock Hill leads up onto the moor again on the road back to County Gate. **Culbone** Church lays claim to being

Allerford packhorse bridge

opposite: Selworthy

England's smallest; it is best reached by walking, being just over a mile from Porlock Weir or 4 miles from County Gate along the Coast Path. Along the A39 between the top of Porlock Hill and County Gate are several parking spaces with attendant viewpoints.

Mention must be made here, of the Two Moors Way footpath. Starting on the southern edge of Dartmoor and crossing Devon, it arrives on Exmoor by way of West Anstey Common and goes on by Hawkridge and Withypool. The walk cosses the River Barle just below Cow Castle to make a wide swing south and west of Simonsbath. It then heads north over Exe Plain to visit Exe Head, the source of the River Exe, Hoar Oak Tree and the ancient forest boundary. The original oak has been replaced by a young tree. This is a good walk and visits some of the wilder parts of the moor. It is, however, only recommended for experienced walkers.

Additional Information

Accommodation

£££ = expensive
££ = moderate
£ = inexpensive
EM = evening meal available

Exmoor

Exmoor House (££, EM)
Wheddon Cross, TA24 7DU
☎ 01643 841432

Westerclose Country House (£££, EM)
Withypool TA24 7QR
☎ 01643 83302

Dulverton

Exton House Country Hotel (££, EM)
Exton, TA22 9JT
☎ 01643 85635

Dunster

Yarn Market Hotel (££, EM)
25 High Street, TA24 6SF
☎ 01643 821425

Exmoor House Hotel (££, EM)
12 West Street, TA24 6SN
☎ 01643 821268

Minehead

Channel House Hotel (£££, EM)
Church Path, off Northfield Road,
TA24 5QG
☎ 01643 703229

Kildare Lodge (££)
Townsend Road, TA24 5RQ
☎ 01643 702009

Mr & Mrs Smith (£, EM)
Fernside, The Holloway, TA24 5PB
☎ 01643 707594

Watchet

Green Bay (£, EM)
Washford, TA23 0NN
☎ 01984 40303

Places to Visit

Dunster

Dunster Castle (NT)
☎ 01643 821314
Garden & park open: daily,
February-March, October to early
December 11am-4pm; April-
September 11am-5pm.

Castle open: Saturday-Wednesday, April-September 11am-5pm; October 11am-4pm. Good Friday only gardens open.
Mill open: April-June, September & October Sunday-Friday 11am-5pm; open Easter Saturday. July & August daily 11am-5pm.

Minehead

Somerset Farm Park
Allerford
Open: March-October daily 10.30am-4.30pm.

West Somerset Railway
☎ 01643 704996
☎ 01643 707650 (talking timetable)
Open: May-September daily; March-April & October Tuesday-Thursday, Saturday & Sunday; November Sunday; December Saturday & Sunday; Xmas to New Year daily.
Passenger services from Minehead to Bishops Lydeard near Taunton.

Monksilver

Combe Sydenham Country Park
☎ 01984 656284
Courtroom & gardens open: Easter-October, Monday-Friday 1.30-4pm.
Country park open: Easter-October, Sunday-Friday 10am-5pm; November 10am-4pm.

Watchet

Cleeve Abbey
☎ 01984 40377
Open: April-September daily 10am-6pm, October daily 10am-4pm, November-March Wednesday-Sunday 10am-4pm.

Watchet Museum
☎ 01643 2624 for opening hours.

Williton

Orchard Mill Museum
☎ 01984 632133
Open: March-October, Tuesday-Sunday.

Wiveliscombe

Gaulden Manor
Tolland
☎ 01984 667213.
Open: first Sunday in May to first Sunday in September, Sunday & Thursday 2-5.30pm, also Bank Holidays. Parties by appointment.

Tourist Information Centres

Minehead
17 Friday Street
☎ 01643 702624

Dulverton
☎ 01398 23841

Dunster
Dunster Steep
☎ 01643 821835

South Somerset & West Dorset

Milborne Port

Tintinhull
Conservation Worldwide
Trent
Sherborne
Montacute House
Purse Caundle Manor
Ham Hill
YEOVIL
Bradford Abbas
Merriott
Sutton Bingham Reservoir
Yetminster
Crewkerne
Broadwindsor
Evershot
Pilsdon Pen
Beaminster
Parnham House
Cattistock
Lambert's Castle
Whitechurch Canonicorum
Mapperton House
Uplyme
Chideock
Powerstock
Charmouth
Bridport
Lyme Regis
West Bay
Burton Bradstock
Dorchester

N
W   E
S

0   5 miles
0   8 km

A37 A303 A359 A30 A3030 A352 A356 A37 A3066 A35 B3165

opposite: Sherborne

Dorset is noted for its fossils

South Somerset & West Dorset

5

The landscape here is rolling hills, higher in the southern half on the Dorset Downs. The main A30 goes through the northern section and the A35 near the coast. The A37 runs from Yeovil to Dorchester with the A356 from Crewkerne joining near Dorchester. There are plenty of minor roads as well, avoiding the busy main routes. Starting near Milborne Port the area is described in a clockwise direction. Using a base for a few days, say Sherborne or Yeovil, then Beaminster or Bridport for a day or so it is possible, without too much daily travel, to make short forays into the outlying areas.

Being within a couple of miles of Sherborne, Milborne Port and the nearby village of **Purse Caundle** just get into this chapter. The beautiful small manor house in Purse Caundle lies close by the stream flowing down and feeding into Sherborne Lake. It is a fifteenth-century house with changes made in Tudor times, and is open to the public on certain days. In the drawing room is an oriel window looking out to the village street. A well in the hall has walls reaching up the stairs, no doubt a device built in case of siege. King John gave the manor and lands to a man who cared for the hounds used when hunting in the nearby Blackmoor Vale. The roof of the hall is original. The church is also fifteenth century and has an embattled tower; the high chancel arch is panelled giving a beautiful effect. In the manor chapel, resting on a desk, is the great Bible brought here during the reign of Charles I. It was chained to the lectern for 250 years then removed, but after 50 years it was returned to its present resting place.

Milborne Port is a modest town just inside Somerset, formerly more important than it is now. Its church is a mixture of Saxon and Norman. There is an old Guildhall to remind us of its former glory in the days when two members of parliament were returned by the town.

Sherborne could have a chapter all to itself. The history of the town goes back more than a thousand years, and it claims to be the loveliest town in Dorset. Surrounded by wooded hills with its lake, deer park and quaint old streets to explore, it is a gem. Among the modern attractions are an open-air swimming pool, tennis, fishing and an eighteen-hole golf course just over a mile north of the town. Half-day closing is Wednesdays.

The thousand-year history of Sherborne has seen many famous men. The Saxon Bishop Aldhelm came from Malmesbury to build a church and found the famous school in the eighth century. King Alfred may have received part of his education here, and his two brothers, both kings before Alfred, are buried here. Sir Walter Raleigh owned the estate, which was given to him by Queen Elizabeth I. Sir Walter decided that he needed a new house, and that is why Sherborne has two 'castles', the medieval one and the 'new' one. It is here that the story began that every school child knows; Raleigh was sitting on a seat in the garden of his new house smoking when his servant, thinking he was on fire, threw a bucket of water over him.

The sixteenth-century castle passed to the Digby family in 1617 and, still owned by them, is open to the public from Easter to September. There is the Lakeside Tea Room for refreshments if you wander from the ruins of the original twelfth-century castle, destroyed by Cromwell, to the new castle. This will have to be by road, as there is no footway between the two. The new castle was enlarged in 1625 and again in 1766 when its gardens were landscaped by 'Capability' Brown. There are 20 acres of lakeside lawns and wooded walks to enjoy. In the castle is a fine collection of pictures with other treasures collected by the Digby family over the last 300 years. A museum of local history is housed in what was the abbey gatehouse, open daily from April to October. Exhibits range from brass rubbings and steam pumps to displays showing the history of Sherborne Silk Mill. There are medieval almshouses in the town, and a lovely structure just near the museum which was built as the monks' washing place.

Goathill, a tiny hamlet just over 2 miles east, has two ghosts — a dog comes down the hill towards Milborne Port and an old lady complete with bonnet and basket has been seen on the road near the Lodge. Sandford Orcas Manor, to the north of Sherborne, is famous for ghosts, harbouring at least twenty, so it is said!

Two miles from Sherborne just off the A30 Yeovil road at **Over Compton**, is Compton House, a sixteenth-century manor house, now the home of Conservation Worldwide. Visitors can see what is being done to improve the environment and visit the 'indoor jungle' where butterflies live in near-natural conditions. Their breeding houses can be seen, also the process of producing thread from the cocoons to make the unique English silk.

The next village north, **Trent**, has the interesting church of St Andrew. It has a medieval spire, but much renovation was done in the early 1840s. Of the buildings round the village many date from the fifteenth and sixteenth centuries. Trent also has a ghost, or ghosts. At Trent Barrow, a mile east of the village, there was a deep pit, into which a coach plunged one dark and dirty night, complete with horses and passengers. Since then cries for help and the sound of galloping horses have been heard — on suitably dark nights of course. Lord Fisher of Lambeth lived at Trent Rectory after he retired in 1962 and officiated as curate in the church. He is buried in the churchyard. King Charles II, fleeing from the Battle of Worcester, was hidden at Trent for three weeks by Sir Frances Wyndham in a secret room in the manor house.

One mile south of the A30 is **Bradford Abbas**, where the church of St Mary Virgin is well worth a visit. There is a fifteenth-century panelled roof supported by angels, many carved bench ends and a Jacobean pulpit. The font is over five hundred years old with four carved figures supporting the corners. The remains of a preaching cross stand in the churchyard. Land nearby was given in AD933 by King Alfred to Sherborne Abbey. The monks had a moated farm which is now called Wyke Farm (not open to view).

Yeovil is a moderately sized town set in pleasant countryside. The modern features of the town are an eighteen-hole golf course, bowls and tennis, fishing and an indoor swimming pool. There is an outdoor recreation centre and a cinema. Many people have heard the name of the town in connection with Westlands, who started manufacturing propeller aircraft and are now world famous for helicopters. This brings Yeovil right up to date, but it was a settlement in Roman times before being deserted in the Dark Ages. Some claim that the names Yeovil and Ilchester have the same Saxon origin. As the Romans built the road from Ilchester to Dorchester, now the A37, on which Yeovil stands, and the Roman settlement was abandoned perhaps the Saxons mixed them up.

On the A359 at the northern end of the town is the old Hundred Stone, probably marking the former parish, and hundred, boundary. There are good views from here north over the Somerset Plain to the Mendips and Glastonbury Tor. In the old days floods in winter often reached from Yeovil to the sea along the River Yeo. The waters have been tamed a little but not entirely — floods came a long way inland in the winter of 1981 when the sea defences at Burnham-on-Sea were breached during a violent westerly gale. Water-borne traffic certainly came as far as Ilchester and maybe further before the railways, and Yeovil received and sent goods by boat via the River Yeo and Bridgwater.

Montacute House

Tintinhull House

The parish church of St John the Baptist was rebuilt in the fourteenth century from local stone from Ham Stone Quarries. Little remains of the original medieval fittings. The church has been likened to other famous churches, though on a smaller scale, notably the famous St Mary Redcliffe at Bristol, and the nave has been compared with Canterbury Cathedral. It contains a brass lectern dating from 1450. Leather work played an important part in the history of the town; the Wyndham Museum has exhibits of domestic and agricultural interest as well as historical and archaeological exhibits. The museum also features the Bailward collection of costumes as well as displays of glass and photographs.

At **Sparkford** near Yeovil is the Haynes Motor Museum, with over 200 rare and beautiful classic motor cars and cycles.

Four miles west of Yeovil on the A3088 is an area to fill a few days. First is **Montacute House**, begun in the sixteenth century and completed in 1600 by Sir Edward Phelips, Speaker of the House of Commons under James I. The house has an H-shaped ground plan, and the local Ham Hill stone was used for its construction. It features balustraded parapets and fluted angle columns. Inside is fine seventeenth- and eighteenth-century furniture, and Elizabethan and Jacobean portraits in the Long Gallery. Picnics are permitted in the car park area and teas are available in the tea room from April to September. The estate, which is now a National Trust property, is over 300 acres and in the gardens are two pavilions which are among the best garden features of the period. The house takes its name from the nearby St Michael's Hill, an ancient earthwork with a folly on the top.

Just over a mile north-west is **Tintinhull House** where there is a delightful small garden within the 4 acres of National Trust Property. They were presented to the Trust in 1953 by Mrs P. E. Reiss who was mainly responsible for the gardens as they appear now.

A mile west along the A3088 from Montacute is the village of **Stoke-sub-Hamdon**, where the fourteenth-century priory is also a National Trust property. The Great Hall is open to the public and was a former residence of the priests of the chantry of St Nicholas. South of the main road is Hamdon Hill, or Ham Hill. Its Iron Age hillfort is one of the largest hilltop enclosures in Britain. The walk round the outer ramparts is nearly 3 miles and over two hundred acres are enclosed. The walk gives extensive views over the surrounding countryside. It was an important site, placed midway between Cadbury Castle and Castle Neroche near Taunton. The Romans used the hill as a fortified position, as it overlooks the Fosse Way. Its fate during the Dark Ages is unknown, but it was used again in Saxon times. There is a war memorial on the hill at the point nearest the main road. Adjoining the main hill is St Michael's Hill, but there is now no sign of the Norman castle that was built there.

The grey-gold stone from the workings of Ham Hill has been used for building locally for literally thousands of years, from the days when the ancient Britons first started to carve out the ramparts up to very recent times. The Roman ramparts and buildings were probably fairly extensive and when the Romans left the site the locals helped themselves to the ready-cut stone from them. When the ready made supplies ran out and serious quarrying began is a little obscure, but throughout the Middle Ages generations of quarrymen lived in the surrounding villages. The area has now been made into the Ham Hill County Park, and the land inside the ramparts has been left a maze of hillocks, ravines, terraces and ridges, a delight for children to explore after picnicking. The hillfort can claim to be unique as there is an inn within the ramparts.

Back on the road, towards Yeovil and south of the main A3088, is the village of **Brympton**. The Norman manor house of Brympton d'Evercy has sixteenth- and seventeenth-century additions. The gardens, stables, church and dower house form a nice grouping.

Naturally it is built of Ham stone and the south front was designed by Inigo Jones. Unfortunately it is no longer open to the public.

South-west from here is **Crewkerne**. There are some quaint old corners to explore in this ancient market town. The parish church of St Bartholomew is one of the finest of the many fifteenth-century churches in the surrounding area. Crewkerne is a blend of Celtic and Saxon names which gives an idea of the age of the place as a settlement. In Saxon times there was a mint in the town. As in many of the surrounding towns and villages clothiers worked in the town, and serge was made here for the East India Company. Sails used on HMS *Victory* at the Battle of Trafalgar were made here. The records of the year 1830 note that the sailcloth-makers of the town made £50,000 from the trade.

Three miles south of Crewkerne on the B3165 is **Clapton**, and the village of **Wayford** where the gardens of Wayford Manor are open to the public.

From the junction of the B3165 and B3164, just over a mile east is Pilsdon Pen with its tumuli and hillfort. This is the highest hill in Dorset, 277m (999ft). From the top of the hill there are good views all round, especially across Marshwood Vale and down the valley of the River Char towards Charmouth and Lyme Bay, both hidden by the hills. Back on the B3165, a mile southwards from Marshwood is another giant hillfort, Lamberts Castle, nearly half a mile long. It is another National Trust property as is the attendant, but smaller, Coneys Castle just to the south on the minor road.

Another mile along the road is a turning south on a minor road leading to the forest park, forest trail and picnic site at Wootton Hill. Though the village of Powerstock is over 10 miles away to the east the forest at one time must have covered much of the area in between. From here it is only about 4 miles to Lyme Regis.

There is much to do and to see in and around **Lyme Regis**. This delightful seaside resort town really can claim to have everything. It is set against a well wooded background with the valley of the River Lym leading back inland to the village of **Uplyme**. Uplyme covers a large area for a village and is the centre for many walks — it is, for example, possible to walk back to Lyme Regis along the river. The Bridle Path Riding Centre offers tuition and accompanied rides.

The attractions offered by Lyme Regis are extensive and range from quiet gardens to deep sea fishing. If you wish to keep your feet on dry land, it is possible to catch a conger eel from the harbour walls. One of the largest fish tanks in Britain can be seen at the aquarium on Victoria Pier, where there are exhibits of local marine

Lyme Regis

Regency cottages on the seafront

life. The sailing club headquarters are also on Victoria Pier, and races are organized at weekends. The bowling green on Monmouth Beach is open to the public, there is a mini-golf course and also a putting green in Langmoor Gardens.

During the summer season local bands play on the Marine Parade and there are displays by Morris Men and folk dance societies. The eighteen-hole golf course stands just to the north-east on Timber Hill. Lyme Regis has a champion town crier, and the ancient tradition has been maintained continuously by the town for a thousand years. There is a cinema in Broad Street, and the Marine Theatre offers a variety of entertainment. The Philpot Museum, near the Guildhall, has an interesting collection depicting the town's history, as well as geology, fossils and lace exhibits. Fossils are also displayed at Dinosaurland, housed in a former Congregational Church, where some of the best of the more recent finds are housed. There is a good collection of fossilised molluscs and ammonites and a complete skeleton of a plesiosaurus.

In August is the Regatta, with sand sports and sailing races the week finishes with a Grand Carnival.

Historically the town goes back many centuries; the first settlement is recorded in AD774. For many years the port was one of the most important in England. Medieval records show accounts of ships trading to and from France and later, America. Lyme is recorded in the Domesday Book as having four farms and twenty-six saltmen. In 1284 King Edward I gave the town its charter and 'Regis' was added to its name. Ships from the port took part in the Siege of Calais and the Battle of the Armada. The town was besieged in 1644 during the Civil War by Royalist troops commanded by Prince Maurice, while the Duke of Monmouth landed near Cobb Quay in 1685 to drum up support for his ill-fated rebellion.

As ships grew larger, Lyme Regis declined as a port. However it was saved by its discovery as a watering place; Jane Austen was just one of the many famous people who came to stay.

The parish church of St Michael the Archangel stands on the site of an earlier church. The present building has twelfth-century features but is mainly sixteenth century. Its peal of eight bells contains five of the original six cast in 1770.

The Dorset Coast Path runs from Lyme Regis to Studland. Almost the entire length is within the Dorset Area of Outstanding Natural Beauty. It crosses grass, downland and limestone cliffs to the sand dunes round Poole Harbour. Note that due to the unstable nature of some of the cliffs, landslips may cause diversions to be made.

Among the notable features of the area are the spectacular land-slips, particularly west of the town along the Undercliff, where on Christmas Day 1839, several miles of cliff face crashed down. The deeply-fissured area is now densely overgrown with woodland and wild flowers, but there is a footpath from Lyme Regis to Seaton. Note that there are *no* escape routes from the path, which must be followed to its end, or your steps retraced. As the county boundary is so close to the town the Undercliff is actually in Devonshire, but it is an interesting feature for anyone visiting Lyme Regis.

Charmouth is only 2½ miles along the coast from Lyme Regis; it is an attractive holiday village with a wide main street. There are hotels and shops and a secluded stretch of sandy beach leading to fine shingle. Charmouth was Jane Austen's favourite place.

Many fossils have been found in the cliffs round the Lyme Regis area; in the parish church at Lyme Regis is a window dedicated to Mary Anning, who spent 8 years liberating from the rock the first ichthyosaurus known to science, a fish-lizard 30ft long. She received £23 for the fossil, which now rests in the Natural History Museum in London. Mary Anning received a small annuity from the Government and a place in the history books.

On the sea front at Charmouth is the Heritage Coast Centre with displays and an audio-visual show about the area's fossils and wildlife. Guided fossil-hunting walks are run from the centre.

Between Lyme Regis and Charmouth is the National Trust land known as Black Ven. It stretches from the coast up to Timber Hill and the golf course. In all it is 49 acres, including 29 acres of cliff.

East of Charmouth and stretching to Eype Mouth near Bridport is the vast Golden Cap Estate, nearly 2,000 acres of beach, farmland, hill and cliff. It includes 5 miles of the coast and is served by 15 miles of footpaths including the Coast Path. Golden Cap is the highest cliff on the south coast of England. Car access is permitted to viewpoints at Chardown and Stonebarrow Hill. There is access to much of the estate but visitors are reminded that most of the land consists of working farms and it is important that crops are not damaged and stock not disturbed. Also, the preservation of plants and wildlife must be considered. The Anchor Inn at **Seatown** through Chideock, where there is car access to the sea, will provide a lunch stop. **Chideock**, a very pretty village, has two inns, an hotel and two churches. It held a castle of which nothing remains today except markings in the field. It was destroyed by order of parliament after the Civil War. There is a Catholic martyr's memorial in Ruins Lane.

Charmouth and Golden Cap

The harbour at West Bay near Bridport

Golden Cap from Seatown

North of the A35 two miles from Charmouth is the village of **Whitechurch Canonicorum**. Here, at the church of St Candida and The Holy Cross, is the thirteenth-century shrine to the saint, who is also known as St Wite. Very little is known about her, but she may have been a Saxon woman killed during the Danish raid. Through the three holes in the front of the tomb pilgrims could put injured limbs for healing. This is one of the few remaining churches in Britain to retain relics of a saint.

To the west is the town of **Bridport**, which is full of history. Among the many old buildings is the handsome Georgian town hall and the street going south from here has some interesting old houses, including the Priors' House dating from the Middle Ages. The town has many buildings from the seventeenth, eighteenth and nineteenth centuries. The museum and art gallery in South Street has collections of local history, rural life, geology, natural history and a doll collection. Bridport has a carnival week in late August, and a one-day real ale festival (enquire locally for details).

In the parish church traces of the original thirteenth-century building can be found. Joan of Navarre arrived in Bridport in 1403 on the way to her wedding with Henry IV. King Charles II had a narrow escape from Cromwell's men in the town and a notice at the corner of the lane leading to Dorchester marks the escape route.

Ropes have been made in the town since the thirteenth century. King John ordered ship's cables from Bridport, and ropes from the town used by hangmen were called 'Bridport Daggers'. In the time of Henry VIII an Act of Parliament showed that the Royal Navy had used Bridport ropes from time immemorial. The most famous son of the town was the Bishop of Salisbury known as Giles of Bridport.

A programme of guided walks in the area is displayed in the information office window. Bridport is one end of the Dorset Downs Walk from Blandford Forum.

Due south of Bridport is **West Bay**, and sitting on top of East Cliff is an eighteen-hole golf course. There is a pleasant cliff top walk from West Bay to Burton Bradstock with a return route via the bridletrack over North Hill, past Bennett Hill Farm to Bothenhampton and so back to West Bay. An evening stroll along the front at West Bay shows up the lights of Lyme Regis to the west and Portland to the east.

In an converted salt house the Harbour Museum tells the story of Bridport's famouse rope and net-making industry and the history of the harbour.

In the nearby village of **Burton Bradstock** is the Old Farming

Collection, with old farm tools and machinery in a lovely setting by the River Bride at Bredy Farm.

From the village of **Pymore**, just north of Bridport on the minor road from near the town hall, it is possible to walk by riverside path to Parnham House, Beaminster. The walk is about 4½ miles, or turn left to Elwell Lodge and return to Pymore on a bridleway over the hill for a round trip of about 6 miles from Bridport.

Eggardon Hill, 5 miles east and north of the A35 near Askerwell, is an ancient hillfort 250m (820ft) high, giving good views of the surrounding countryside. The ramparts of the defensive earthwork are still 9m (30ft) high, and the line of the nearby Roman road to Dorchester is visible. Park in the lane at the foot of the hill, and from the top of the hill it is possible to go by bridleway, south-west to Eggardon Farms turning left at each farm to climb back up to the start. The hill was used in the film version of Thomas Hardy's *Far From The Madding Crowd.*

Powerstock village has a notable church, the chancel having a fine Norman arch. On either side of the late fifteenth-century doorway a figure stands in a niche. It has been suggested that the male figure is King Wenceslas and the female one St Elizabeth, Princess of Hungary. It is believed that King Athelstan had a palace here, the signs of which remain as an earthwork.

Opposite the church is a small lane leading to a bridleway beside the river. It can be followed to **West Milton**, a mile away. Here there is a new church, built a century ago to replace the old one. Nothing but the fifteenth-century tower remains of the old church, close to the bridleway from Powerstock. By road it is just up the turning signposted to Leigh (no through road) from the bottom of West Milton village.

Mapperton was the next village north, but during the plague of the seventeenth century the entire population of the village was wiped out. The manor house with its adjoining church is all that remains. The terraced hillside gardens are open from March to October on weekday afternoons. There is a series of stepped ponds in the formal gardens and a seventeenth-century summerhouse, with an orangery at one end which is modern.

Beaminster is about 7 miles north of Bridport on the A3066. The bells of the church play the hymn tune *Hanover* every 3 hours. The church is mainly fifteenth-century with a late Norman font which has a square bowl. Beaminster was Thomas Hardy's 'Emminster' in *Tess of the D'Urbevilles*. Close by the church is a seventeenth-century almshouse, there is a large market place and other interesting buildings. The town was almost destroyed by fire three times, twice in the seventeenth and once in the eighteenth century.

The lane by the church leads on to a footpath south to **Parnham House**, a shorter walk than that from Bridport. It is also accessible from the A3066 a mile south of Beaminster. The house dates from the Middle Ages and was almost entirely rebuilt during the reign of King Henry VIII, being enlarged and embellished in 1910 by John Nash, the great Regency architect. Parnham was the seat of the Strode family for some five hundred years.

Since 1976 it has been the home of John Makepeace, the world-famous designer and maker of fine furniture, while in 1977 the School for Craftsmen in Wood was also established here. Unique pieces of furniture from the John Makepeace Workshops are shown in the main house; the workshops are also open to visitors, who see the craftsmen at work. The school and its workshops are not open to the public, nor is student work shown.

A booklet called *Ten Short Walks Around and Near Beaminster* is available from the information office at Bridport at a modest price.

On the A3066 just over a mile north of the town is the Horn Hill road tunnel, an unusual feature in this countryside. Half a mile east from the tunnel on Buckham Down is a picnic site which offers good

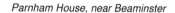

Parnham House, near Beaminster

views northward over the valley of the River Axe. A bridleway goes north from near the picnic site down to the river valley. Turn right and climb back up to Chapel Marsh, rejoin the road and walk down to the car park.

Neaby is Horn Park Gardens with alpine rock gardens, shrub and herbacious borders, terraces and water gardens open to the public.

Just off the A37 Dorchester to Yeovil road on the way north are two interesting churches. The first is at **Cattistock** in the valley of the River Frome. Its handsome church 'would fit a town'. People used to gather on the surrounding hills to hear the carillon of thirty-five bells, the first of its kind in England. A mystery fire in 1940 damaged the tower and melted the bells, but the tower was painstakingly rebuilt in its former style. A former parson established a pack of hounds and started the Cattistock Hunt.

At **Yetminster**, on the other side of the A37, the church of St Andrew was originally consecrated in 1310 and retains most of the original twelve crosses that marked the consecration. Most of the church is fifteenth century, the original roof and paintings are still retained. Two miles south, just through **Leigh**, is a miz-maze. Only a mound now remains, but the young men of the village used to recut the paths every year. Originally raised in prehistoric times, possibly as a ritual site, it was also, supposedly, a witches' meeting place. In the seventeenth century the last witch burned in England was arrested here and executed at Maumbury Rings, Dorchester.

Crossing the A37 again there is a riding establishment at Hillside Saddlery on the road towards Sutton Bingham reservoir.

Penwood Forest Park and forest trail lie about 3 miles due south of West Coker and the main A30 road. The trail is steep in places, but offers good views to the north and east towards Somerset and the town of Yeovil. The Somerset-Dorset border crosses the top of the hill. The trail has a mixture of old natural woodland and young beech, larch, pine and fir; it passes a badger set and a pond.

Sutton Bingham Reservoir completes the tour of this area. It is due south of Yeovil and can be reached from the A37, situated in gentle hills with the county boundary crossing the water. This attractive reservoir is well over a mile long and 142 acres in extent. There is a sailing club on the northern bank and the sailing area covers the northern arms and a little way down the southern stretch of the water. The waters are stocked with brown and rainbow trout for fly fishing. A pleasant viewing and picnic area is provided with toilets and is fenced off from the water for security. The picnic site faces the sailing club so there are usually boats to watch.

Additional Information

Accommodation
£££ = expensive
££ = moderate
£ = inexpensive
EM = evening meal available

Bridport
Roundham House Hotel (££, EM)
Roundham Gardens,
West Bay Road, DT6 4BD
☎ 01308 422753

Britmead House (££)
West Bay Road, DT6 4EG
☎ 01308 422941

Rudge Farm (£, EM)
Chilcombe, DT6 4NF
☎ 01308 482630

Crewkerne
The George Hotel (£££, EM)
Market Square, TA18 7LP
☎ 01460 73650

Merefield Vegetarian Guest House (£)
East Street, TA18 7AB

Lyme Regis
Kersbrook Hotel (£££, EM)
Pound Road, DT7 3HX
☎ 01297 442596

Coverdale Guest House (£)
Woodmead Road, DT7 3AB
☎ 01297 442882

Places to Visit

Beaminster
Horn Park Gardens
☎ 01308 862212
Open: April-October Tuesday,
Wednesday, Sunday and Bank
Holidays 2-6pm.

Mapperton House
☎ 01308 862645
Garden open: daily 2-6pm. House
open by appointment only.

Parnham House
☎ 01308 862204
Open: April-October, Sunday,
Wednesday and Bank Holidays
from Good Friday, 10am-5pm.
Parnham College not open to visitors.

Bridport
Bridport Museum
South Street
☎ 01308 422116
Open: April-October Monday-
Saturday 10am-5pm, Sunday 2-
5pm; November-March Wednes-
day & Saturday 10am-5pm,
Sunday 2-5pm.

Harbour Museum
West Bay
☎ 01308 420997
Open: April-September Monday-
Sunday 10am-6pm.

Old Farming Collection
Bredy Farm, Burton Bradstock
☎ 01308 897229
Open: Spring Bank Holiday-
September 10.30am-5.30pm.

Charmouth
Heritage Coast Centre
Lower Sea Lane, DT6 6LL
☎ 01297 560772
Open: Easter, Whitsun-September
& autumn half term, daily 10.30am.

Lyme Regis
Dinosaurland
6a Broad Street
☎ 01297 443541
Open: Easter-October daily, winter
weekends and Christmas holidays.

Marine Aquarium & Cobb History
☎ 01297 443678
Open: Easter-October 10am-5pm.

Philpot Museum
Bridge Street
☎ 01297 443370
Open: April-October daily 10am-5pm, Sunday 10am-12 noon, 2-5pm.

Sherborne
Conservation Worldwide
Compton House, Over Compton
☎ 01935 74608
Open: April-October daily 10am-5pm.

Purse Caundle Manor
☎ 01963 250400
Open: Easter Monday and May-September, Thursday, Sunday and Bank Holiday Monday 2-5pm.

Sandford Orcas Manor
☎ 01963 220206
Open: May-September, Sunday 2-6pm, Monday 10am-6pm and Easter Monday 10am-6pm.

Sherborne Museum
Abbey Gate House
☎ 01935 812252
Open: Easter-October Tuesday-Friday 10.30am-4.30pm, Sunday 2.30-4.30pm.

Sherborne Castle
☎ 01935 813182
Open: Easter-September Thursday, Saturday, Sunday and Bank Holiday Mondays. Castle 1.30-5pm, grounds 12.30-5pm.

Sherborne Old Castle
☎ 01935 812730
Open: April-September daily 10am-6pm, October daily 10am-4pm, November-March Wednesday-Sunday 10am-4pm.

Yeovil
Haynes Motor Museum
Sparkford, BA22 7LH
☎ 01963 440804
Open: daily 9.30am-5.30pm.

Montacute House (NT)
House open: April-October, daily except Tuesday (closed Good Friday), 12noon-5.30pm.
Garden & park open: all year daily except Tuesday 11.30am-5.50pm or dusk if earlier.

Stoke-sub-Hamdon Priory (NT)
Open: daily 10am-6pm or dusk.
The hall of the chantry house only.

Tintinhull House Garden (NT)
Open: April-September, Wednesday-Sunday and Bank Holiday Monday 12 noon-6pm.

Tourist Information Centres

Bridport
32 South Street, DT6 3NQ
☎ 01308 424901

Crewkerne
☎ 01460 77277

Lyme Regis
Church Street, DT7 3BS
☎ 01297 442138

Sherborne
Digby Road, DT9 3NL
☎ 01935 815341

Yeovil
Petters House, Petters Way
☎ 01935 71279

Dorset Downs & Bournemouth

6

Apart from the coastal strip around Poole and Bournemouth, this part of the country seems mostly to have people rushing through to other places, to the coast, to the West Country. But to pause and look round the area can be very rewarding — turning off the beaten track to take the byways can reveal treasure. Not only ancient hillforts or 'big houses' with fine gardens, but also peace and tranquility.

Three major roads radiate from the east. The A30 crosses the northern part going through Shaftesbury. Coming over the downs to Blandford Forum is the A354 on its way from Salisbury to Dorchester. At the end of the M27 is the A31 through the New Forest and Ringwood to Wimborne Minster, while the A338 is a fast route almost to the centre of Bournemouth. A favourite tourist route southwards in summer is the A350 from Wiltshire to Poole.

Many happy hours may be spent walking along green lanes or hill tracks in this part of the country. Three published walks include parts of this region. *A Severn to Solent Walk* comes in from Buckhorn

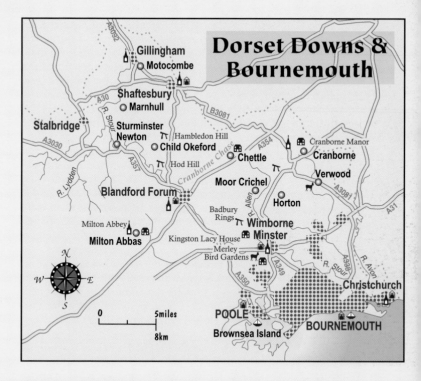

Dorset Downs & Bournemouth

Weston to Gillingham and Shaftsbury, it crosses the Downs and goes through Three Legged Cross to the New Forest at Ringwood. *The Wessex Way* comes in from Wiltshire over Bokerley Dyke going south-west to Spetisbury and Wareham Forest. *A Dorset Downs Walk* starts at Blandford Forum and goes via Milton Abbas to Bridport. Mostly the tracks are deserted, whereas on the Ridgeway or the Pennine Way you will not lack for company.

Gillingham is the most northerly town in Dorset, an ancient place where much history is recorded. Edmund Ironside overtook the fleeing Danes here. The Confessor was proclaimed king after a *Witenagemot*, an Anglo-Saxon national council or parliament, was held here. Sir Walter Raleigh once held the post of Forest Ranger. A grammar school was founded here in 1516 and one ex-headmaster, Robert Frampton, became Bishop of Gloucester. Samuel Pepys declared one of his sermons 'the best he had ever heard'. Our ancient kings had a palace here and the remains of the earthwork can still be seen at the end of Kingscourt Road off the B3081 road to Shaftesbury. The Gillingham Museum tells the story of the town and the surrounding villages from prehistoric times to the present day, including the artist John Constable's association with the area.

Just a little way south is **Motcombe**, a small sleepy village. Outside the church is the stump of an old preaching cross. Preaching crosses were on sites used for worship before a church was built.

South again lies **Shaftesbury**, a magnificent example of a hill town. Founded by King Alfred who began the abbey, the site was certainly in use before that, as traces over 2,000 years old have been found. The abbey was started on the site of a Roman temple and is the burial place of many kings and queens. In those days there were three mints, two hospitals, a thriving market and about a dozen churches. There are seventeenth-century almshouses and an eighteenth-century grammar school.

There are four churches. St Peter's is the oldest, and its medieval walls look down on the High Street. The crypt, which has now been restored, was once used as a store by the landlord of the inn next door. St Rumbold's has a Norman font, St James' has a fine east window and the Victorian Holy Trinity has an effigy which may have come from the abbey.

From Castle Hill the view is south-west to the Vale of Blackmore, and from the terrace walk by the abbey the view is east towards Wiltshire. Gold Hill is an interesting, and very steep, cobbled street.

There was a mayor of Shaftesbury in 1350, and the corporation has a silver seal older than the Spanish Armada. One of the maces in current use dates from 1475.

Once a great procession of all the great nobles of Wessex, led by Archbishop Dunstan, entered Shaftesbury. They bore the body of Edward the Martyr, murdered at Corfe Castle by his stepmother. For a while the young king had been buried at Wareham, then he was brought to a more fitting place for a king to be buried. The nuns guarded the tomb and pilgrims thronged there. The abbey prospered and at its height covered 10 acres. Eventually the abbey fell into ruin and was lost. The plan of the abbey was revealed by painstaking excavation during the 1930s, when a lead casket was found and claimed as the remains of Edward the Martyr. The remains had been hidden by the nuns at the time of the dissolution and subsequently lost for nearly 400 years. The abbey ruins are set in a walled garden with a museum housing excavated artifacts and a model of the town as it was at the time of the Dissolution.

The A30 goes west from Shaftesbury and it is a lovely drive to Milborne Port and Sherborne. South from the crossroads with the A357 is **Stalbridge**. It lies in the Vale of Blackmore, Hardy's 'Vale of Little Dairies', and although the church is fifteenth-century the tower is Victorian. The proudest possession of Stalbridge is the restored fifteenth-century market cross. Once a feature of every town, there are sadly few remaining intact.

Further east on the A357 is **Sturminster Newton**. The twin villages of Sturminster and Newton were divided by the River Stour and joined by a bridge, which is over four hundred years old. Once there were connections with Glastonbury Abbey, hence the 'minster'. The church dates from the fourteenth and fifteenth centuries. This was Thomas Hardy's Stour Castle, and he spent much time here writing his early books. Most of the houses in the market square are Georgian. Sturminster Newton can be reached on foot from the minor road south-east from Stalbridge. Cross the River Lydden at Barber Bridge, and at Manor Farm, where the road bends southerly, keep straight on to join a bridleway which emerges at Newton near the mill.

On the Bath road is an eighteenth-century working watermill, now driven by a turbine dating from 1904, that may be visited.

North from Sturminster Newton on the B3092 is **Marnhull**. Students of Thomas Hardy novels will know that this was the home of Tess of the D'Urbervilles. Overlooking the Vale of Blackmore the village is scattered around a hill. The church stands near the crossroads, has a handsome pinnacled tower and is mostly fourteenth century. The B3092 leads northwards to join the A30 at East Stour where there is a right turn back to Shaftesbury.

South from Shaftesbury the A350 winds between the hills towards Blandford Forum. Two miles before the town the A357 joins. A west turn at the traffic lights leads to Shillingstone and **Child Okeford**. Behind Child Okeford lies Hambledon Hill. A good walk goes up the hill to the Neolithic camp and hillfort. Here are magnificent views all round; south is another prehistoric hillfort on Hod Hill, inside the ramparts of which is a Roman fort.

Across the river and main road are picnic sites near Ibberton, Okeford Fitzpaine and just south of Shillingstone along a by-road signposted to White Pit. The latter is a small secluded site in young beech and oak. South of the site lie Eastcombe Wood, Shillingstone Hill, Blandford Forest and Bonsley Common. Splendid walks crisscross through the woods, mostly tracks which are designated as bridleways; they are rather confusing so be careful not to get lost.

Blandford Forum lies to the south of Cranborne Chase and at the eastern end of the Dorset downland. Both the A354 Salisbury to Dorchester and the A350 Poole to Shaftesbury roads pass through the town. Its Georgian appearance is mainly due to a fire which, in the eighteenth century, destroyed the old town.

Blandford is a good town to wander around. There is The Old House built for the German-born Dr Sagittary in 1661. Up the hill on the way to Salisbury are the Ryves Almshouses, built in 1682. Alfred Stevens the sculptor was born in the town.

The Bastard brothers, born in Blandford Forum, were responsible for many buildings in the surrounding area, both houses and churches. At the end of the Market Place is John Bastard's pump and fire monument. It has an inscription, which thanks Divine Providence 'which raised this town like a Phoenix from its ashes, to its present beautiful and flourishing state'. The monument stands in front of the Church of St Peter and St Paul which was built in 1733, also by the Bastard brothers. Opposite the church is the local museum with displays of the town's life, industry and culture.

Lace was made in the town until 1811. Blandford bone lace was considered by Daniel Defoe to be as fine as any he had seen. Button making was a Dorset cottage industry, and Blandford was no exception. At one time there were four button makers in the Market Place. In 1770, for instance, the inhabitants of Blandford Forum workhouse, three men and eleven women, made fifteen gross of large and small buttons in the month of June.

The Charles I held a series of reviews all over Dorset and the 700-strong First Battalion Dorset Volunteers assembled at Blandford Forum for military exercises. In 1831 the Dorset Yeomanry were re-enrolled to cope with riots and unruly behaviour of labourers in pursuit of higher wages. At the Blandford Army Camp is the Royal Signals Museum telling the story of the communications vital to any army, from flags to World War II radio equipment.

At the very western edge of the town lie green meadows alongside the River Stour. On the opposite bank is the steep wooded slope named 'The Cliff', at the northern end of which is Bryanston School. Built for Viscount Portman in 1890, it became a school in 1927. The fortunes of the Portman family changed, according to superstition, when they caused the old house to be pulled down to build the new one. In doing so they disturbed the ghost of 'Aunt Charlotte'. It has also been reported that sometimes the lodge gates would open and a phantom coach would go up the drive. Another legend was that if

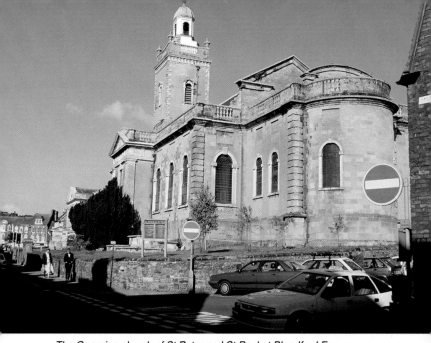

The Georgian church of St Peter and St Paul at Blandford Forum

The impressive Iron Age hillfort of Badbury Rings

the peacocks left Bryanston the Portmans would soon follow. Soon after the peacocks were sold the third Viscount died and the family sold the house and part of the estate.

Milton Abbas lies 6 miles south-west, or 7 miles if you follow the Dorset Downs Walk. Milton Abbey was founded in 932 by King Athelstan as a college of canons; it later became a Benedictine monastery. A school, which had about seventy pupils, was closed towards the end of the eighteenth century following objections from the Earl of Dorchester as it was too close to his house. Among his objections he included an assault on the character of the school's headmaster. It was alleged that he had allowed the school building to deteriorate to the point at which it was unsafe for the pupils. The poor headmaster had evidently used his floorboards and doors as fuel! His Grace also complained that the boys climbed over his walls to steal fruit and eggs. Thomas Masterman Hardy, Admiral Nelson's Flag Captain, was one of the supposed ring leaders.

The main building is a school now, the buildings are in better repair, and no doubt the pupils are better behaved. The Abbey Church may be visited, as may the Abbots Hall and parts of Abbey House during the school holidays.

Near the abbey church is a map of the old village. The new village was built in 1771 by Lord Dorchester, not just another village moved at the whim of a rich landowner. It took that gentleman twenty years to acquire the houses of the old village as they fell vacant. It took some litigation as well — one owner accused his Lordship of flooding him out. A new church was built for the villagers using stone from the old tithe barn. This was possibly one of the first attempts at building a model village. The 'new' village is very pleasant and caters for tourists by way of a gift shop, art exhibition and rural life museum.

St Catherine's Chapel stands in the woods above the abbey church. A flight of grass steps leads up to it and from the chapel there is a splendid view of Milton Abbey church. St Catherine's was originally a Saxon chapel. Its varied career includes rebuilding by the Normans, and a period as a labourer's cottage before it became a workshop and finally a store. It has been repaired and restored.

North-east of Blandford Forum stretches a beautiful area of wooded hills and valleys, which runs into Wiltshire. This is **Cranborne Chase**. A chase was a hunting ground held by a non-royal personage, whereas a forest was a hunting ground held by the Crown. Cranborne was a favourite of King John who was reputed to have favoured a white stag and forbade anyone else to hunt it.

The chase lies between the A350 and the A354. To the south-east of the A354 is an area of low downland stretching into Ringwood Forest, an area rich in historic remains. At the southern end of the B3082 Blandford Forum to Wimborne Minster road is **Badbury Rings**, a gigantic hillfort dominating the surrounding countryside. There is ample space to park and stroll round. Bridleways go north-east from each side of the Rings joining near Kings Down Farm, a stroll of nearly two miles. Badbury Rings stands at the site of a Roman crossroads. At the northern end is the Dorset Cursus, two parallel banks about 74m (80yd) apart and over 6 miles in length. The whole area is rich in archaeological sites, barrows, ditches and tracks abound, and it is a fine area for walking. The Roman road running south to Badbury Rings is known as Ackling Dyke. Bokerley Dyke forms part of the Wiltshire border, a huge earthwork across the line of the Roman road. It was built about the fourth century AD to fill in a gap between two forested sections, and to protect north Dorset from invasion.

Two miles east of the Cursus is the small village of **Chettle**. Close to the church is the elegant mellow brick and stone Chettle House, built between 1710 and 1720 by the Bastard brothers for George Chafin who was then ranger of Cranborne Chase. House and gardens are open.

Along the B3081 to the south-east is **Cranborne**, a lovely village in a superb setting of woods and hills. The twelfth-century church of Saint Mary and Saint Bartholomew has a massive church tower and traces of medieval wall painting. The church was built on the foundations of a monastery, where there was once a Saxon church. Cranborne Manor, behind the church, is a building of grey stone, mostly Tudor with older parts. It is surrounded by lovely walled gardens, laid out by John Tradescant, with a lawn and yew hedges. There is a fine beech avenue in front of the house. King Charles I slept at the manor in 1644. Only the gardens are open.

For a walk of just over 3 miles from just beyond Cranborne church take the road to Cranborne Farm for a mile. Turn north-east on a track and when you meet the next track, at a T junction, turn right and follow it to a minor road and back to Cranborne.

On the B3078 going south towards Wimborne Minster is Knowlton Circles, a Bronze Age henge, a sacred place over 4,000 years old. In this area, so rich in ancient remains, there were many barrows and three henges or circles. Most have been ploughed away but much remains. The church stands in a circle 92m (100yd) in diameter. Roofless for years, the walls are complete, a mixture of sandstone, limestone and flint. It is fourteenth or fifteenth century, but of unknown dedication. The village which the church served has completely disappeared.

At the next crossroads south stands Horton Inn. To the south-east is **Horton**, while above the village is Horton Tower. It can be reached on foot: follow the footpath sign to Horton Heath, then go right through a gate at the head of the road near a house entrance. The brick-built tower was erected in the mid-eighteenth century for Humphrey Sturt of Horton Manor. It was built as an observatory, but whether for observing stars or deer is in doubt. Sadly it is slowly falling apart. None of the interior floors remain and it is a very odd looking structure. It is a pleasant walk past the tower into Ferndown Forest, half a mile away, but you will have to retrace your steps.

On down the B3078 is **Wimborne Minster**. The minster has a history going back to Saxon times, with a noted lantern tower, a rare chained library and an eight-hundred-year-old font. A wooden quarter jack still stands outside, after centuries, striking the hours. There is the thirteenth-century St Margarets Hospital Chapel. Deans Court gardens are open on certain Sundays and bank holidays. The

Wimborne Minster

The Egyptian obelisk at Kingston Lacy

Priest's House Museum of East Dorset Life is a must for visitors. Wimborne is the burial place of Ethelred, the elder brother of Alfred the Great, who himself was here many times. This was the site of Alfred's defeat by the Danes, when they burnt the town and he fled to the Somerset moors to gain his fame by burning the cakes. About 200yd west of the minster is the Model Town and Gardens.

Just south of Wimborne Minster at **Merley** and signposted off the A31/A349 junction are Merley Bird Gardens, set in a lovely historic walled garden with an alpine rockery and a herb garden. There are all kinds of birds from parrots to penguins, a pets corner, a picnic site, a children's play area and other entertainments.

Quite close by is Merley House, a fine mansion built in 1750 by Ralph Willett. There are very fine Georgian plaster ceilings and a beautiful wooden staircase. The house contains some 5,000 model toy cars, ships, aeroplanes and racing cars through the ages.

To the east along the A3l, but to the north of that road, is an area that must be explored. At the eastern end is Ringwood, over the border in Hampshire, while at the western end is Horton. Though outside the modern New Forest it is very much the same sort of country, perhaps a little less wild. On Holt Heath you could well imagine you were in the New Forest though the present boundary is twelve miles away. It was to Holt Lodge that the Duke of Monmouth was taken after his capture on Holt Heath.

One and a half miles north-west of Wimborne Minster is **Kingston Lacy House**, an imposing seventeenth-century house designed by Sir Roger Pratt. It was remodelled in 1835 by Sir Charles Barry and clad in Chilmark stone. It houses one of the finest picture collections in Britain and a small collection of ancient Egyptian artifacts. The extensive gardens include Lime Walk, Laurel Walk and Cedar Avenue, a fernery and a sunken garden.

From Wimborne Minster a minor road goes through the Colehill area to Broom Hill. Nearly a mile further on is a car park for White Sheet Plantation picnic site, a sheltered place in mature pine woods. There are attractive walks nearby.

Continue on the minor road to Three Legged Cross, then join the B3072 to go north to **Verwood**. Just to the north of Verwood and the B3081 is the Dorset Heavy Horse Centre. Here there are Clydesdales, Suffolk Punch, Percheron, Shires, the only Canadian-Belgian horses in Europe, miniature ponies, wild fowl and bird aviaries. There are horse parades mornings and afternoons.

The major conurbation is **Bournemouth** — a seaside town *par excellence*, and neighbouring **Poole**. What can one say about a place that has everything? Seven miles of golden beaches bordered by promenades and sandstone cliffs. The cliffs are broken by deep valleys, the famous 'chines', filled with pine trees, that give access to the beach. There are two piers: Bournemouth pier has a Pier Theatre which offers traditional entertainment in the summer season, while Boscombe pier has an amusement hall at the seaward end. Bournemouth pier has cruise launches and fishing.

There are no less than five cinemas in Bournemouth, and three theatres. The theatres offer traditional farce, a symphony orchestra, opera, musicals, drama, ballet and pantomime. The list of night-clubs seems endless and there are even four casinos.

As befits a town of its size Bournemouth is an excellent shopping centre. Westover Road is known as the 'Bond Street' of Bournemouth for the large number of quality shops. Four Victorian arcades enhance the town and Boscombe and Pokesdown are renowned for their antique shops. Similarly, Poole has the Arndale Centre with a wide range of shops, restaurants and coffee bars under one roof.

The area offers sports of all kinds, including ten-pin bowling, ice skating, and roller skating. The large indoor heated swimming pool has diving facilities and seats for 700 spectators. There are also pools at Poole, Christchurch and Kinson.

There are seven squash centres, twelve tennis clubs, eight putting greens, and no less than eleven golf courses in an 11-mile radius.

Tuition and hire facilities for windsurfing are available at Poole, as are facilities for water skiing. It is also possible to have tuition in sailing from one of the many sailing schools around the Poole area. Not only is Poole Harbour almost completely landlocked, so it is comparatively safe, it is also sheltered from the west by the Purbeck Hills. It is reputed to be the second largest harbour in the world, and is particularly beautiful with a number of creeks and islands.

Of course, at a seaside resort with boats coming in to the pier and a harbour close by there is sea fishing on offer. Poole harbour has a regular boat service, round Brownsea Island or out to the beaches at Sandbanks. Freshwater fishing is available close by on the River Stour or the Hampshire Avon, which join just behind Hengistbury Head, to the east of the town.

For the really energetic Hengistbury Head has a fitness circuit — a sort of minor assault course with exercises to do. If that does not tire you out, in Meyrick Park on Central Drive there is a 2½-mile cross-country track round a golf course. There is bowling, croquet, pitch and putt, crazy golf, mini-golf, cycle speedway and large 2m x 2m (6ft x 6ft) outdoor chess boards at the end of the pier. There are six sport centres, model boat sailing and a model car racing circuit. An outdoor model railway offers rides on Bank Holidays and Sunday afternoons and there is a very large indoor model layout.

There are a number of museums in the area. The Russell-Cotes Art Gallery and Museum is in an extravagant Italianate seaside villa on a fine cliff-top location. Sir Merton Russell-Cotes journeyed far and wide and built up an extensive collection that he left, with his home, to the people of Bournemouth. The museum includes a spectacular collection of Victorian and Edwardian paintings, as well as sculptures, decorative art, furniture, modern art and Buddhist shrines.

The Shelley Rooms in Boscombe Manor is devoted to the Romantic poet Percy Bysshe Shelley. It is housed in two rooms at Shelley Park which was once the home of the poet's son.

At the top of the Old Christchurch road pedestrian zone is the ExpoCentre where there are three exhibitions. Dinosaur Safari not only has real fossils and rare casts, but uses reconstructions, computer simulations and audio-visual displays to show what it was like when dinosaurs ruled the earth. Mummies and Magic shows the secrets of the royal mummies of ancient Egypt, while the Bournemouth Bears takes a nostalgic look at the world of teddy bears.

Poole's museums reflect the life and history of the town. The Waterfront Museum illustrates the town's industries and the association with the sea from prehistoric times until early this century, as well as the story of Scouting. In the same building near the quay Scaplens Court Museum looks at domestic history and childhood.

Nearby on Poole Quay is the Aquarium Complex where you can see freshwater and marine species of fish, both local and tropical, as well as snakes, crocodiles, insects, spiders and amphibians.

Overlooking Poole harbour is Compton Acres which includes a Japanese garden, Italian garden, rock garden, water garden, heather dell and woodland walk as well as many pieces of fine sculpture.

As a family resort Bournemouth has plenty of facilities for children. There are six children's playgrounds, five amusement areas and three children's parks. There are paddling pools, an aviary, Noddy trains and trampolines.

There is a team of lively and enthusiastic experts waiting to take you on a conducted walking tour of the town. Their knowledge of the town is prodigious and they have some interesting stories on subjects like the first resident, the smugglers, or just where to go shopping. A modest charge is made; the walks start most days at the tourist information centre, Westover Road, and last about 1½ hours.

In Poole Harbour is **Brownsea Island**. The island is 500 acres or about 3 miles round, and has been in the hands of the National Trust since 1962. There is nature reserve administered by the Dorset Naturalist Trust. Boats go to the island from Poole Quay or Sandbanks, and it is open to the public between April and the end of September. There are red squirrels, golden pheasants, a colony of terns and a large heronry. Masses of daffodils are the remains of an attempt at commercial flower growing.

Historically Brownsea Island can go back to the Romans, King Canute, and Edward the Confessor. At one time it belonged to the monks of Cerne Abbey. Four hundred years ago King Henry VIII built a castle to guard the harbour, but little of the original castle remains, and it is now a holiday home. Modern amenities include an information office, a shop and a restaurant. The first scout camp was

Christchurch Priory

organised on the island by Baden Powell in 1907.

Christchurch, on the border with Hampshire, is now almost a suburb of Bournemouth. There are attractive river frontages to the Stour and Avon, which run into Christchurch Bay and the ruins of a twelfth-century castle. It is the priory church, the longest parish church in England, which dominates. It became the parish church after the priory was dissolved in 1539, and so avoided the fate of so many other religious buildings. There is an impressive thirteenth-century porch, while inside are the characteristic round arches of the earlier Norman period. The tower, which is quite small relative to the rest of the building is from the fifteenth century. The fine fan vaulting and monuments, including one to the poet Shelley, make this one of the best churches in Dorset.

The Red House Museum, in an early eighteenth-century brick building that was once the parish workhouse, has displays of local history, costumes and natural history, as well as marine and fresh-water aquaria. For the more technically minded the old Christchurch Power Station is now a museum of electrical power, with water and steam generators and early domestic appliances.

Additional Information

Accommodation
£££ = expensive
££ = moderate
£ = inexpensive
EM = evening meal available

Blandford Forum
The Talbot Hotel (££, EM)
Iwerne Minster DT11 8QN
☎ 01747 811269

Sturminster Newton
Mr & Mrs Hookham-Bassett (££, EM)
Stourcastle Lodge, Goughs Close
DT10 1BU
☎ 01258 472320

Mr & Mrs Kirby (£, EM)
Droop Farm, Hazelbury Bryan,
DT10 2ED
☎ 01258 817244

Bournemouth
Burley Court Hotel (£££, EM)
Bath Road BH1 2NP
☎ 01202 552824

Carisbrooke Hotel (££, EM)
42 Tregonwell Road, BH2 5NT
☎ 01202 290432

St Michaels Guest House (£, EM)
42 St Michaels Road, Westcliff,
BH2 5DY
☎ 01202 557386

Poole
Fairlight Hotel (££, EM)
1 Golf Links Road, Broadstone,
BH18 8BE
☎ 01202 694316

The Rosemount Hotel (£, EM)
167 Bournemouth Road,
Lower Parkstone, BH14 9HT
☎ 01202 732138

Ferndown

Coach House Inn (££, EM)
579 Wimborne Rd East, BH22 9NW
☎ 01202 861222

Places to Visit

Blandford Forum

Blandford Forum Museum
Bere's Yard, Market Place
Open: April-September Monday-
Saturday 10am-4pm.

Chettle House
☎ 0125 889 209
House and gardens open: April-
October, daily except Tuesday
10.30am-5.30pm.

Royal Signals Museum
Blandford Camp
☎ 01258 482248
Open: all year, Monday-Friday
10am-5pm, also weekends June-
September 10am-4pm.

Bournemouth

Bournemouth Bears
Dinosaur Safari
Mummies & Magic
Expo Centre
Old Christchurch Lane
☎ 01202 293544
Open: daily 9.30am-5.30pm (phone
for winter opening times).

Russell-Cotes Art Gallery & Museum
East Cliff BH1 3AA
☎ 01202 551009/551500
Open: Tuesday-Sunday 10am-5pm.
Admission free Saturday & Sunday.

Shelley Rooms
Beechwood Ave, Boscombe BH5 1NE
☎ 01202 303571
Open Tuesday-Sunday 10am-5pm.
Admission Free.

Christchurch

Red House Museum & Gardens
Quay Road
☎ 01202 482860

Southern Electric Museum
The Old Power Station, Bargates
☎ 01202 480467
Open: Monday-Friday Easter-June
1.30-4pm, July-September 10am-4pm.

Cranborne

Cranborne Manor
☎ 01725 517248
Open: April to September,
Wednesday 9am-5pm.

Gillingham

Museum
Chantry Fields
☎ 01747 822173/823176
Open: Monday, Tuesday, Thursday, Friday 10am-5pm, Saturday
10am-12 noon. Closed Bank
Holidays.

Milton Abbas

Abbey
Church open daily except school
Speach Day (late May) and 25 Dec.

House
☎ 01258 880489
Open during school holidays.

Poole

Aquarium Complex
Hennings Wharf, The Quay
☎ 01202 686712
Open: daily summer 9am-9pm,
spring & autumn 10am-5.30pm,
winter 10am-5pm (5.30pm at
weekends).

Compton Acres Gardens
Canford Cliffs, BH13 7ES
☎ 01202 700778
Open: March-October daily
10.30am-6.30pm (or dusk if earlier).
Last admission 5.45pm.

Poole Pottery
☎ 01202 672866
Open: all year round Monday-
Saturday 10am-5pm and Sunday in
summer.

Waterfront Museum
Scaplens Court Museum
4 High Street, BH15 1BW
☎ 01202 683138
Open: Monday-Saturday 10am-
5pm, Sunday 2-5pm.

Shaftesbury
Abbey Museum
Palk Walk
☎ 01747 852910
Open: April-October daily 10am-
5.30pm.

Local History Museum
Gold Hill
☎ 01747 852157
Open: daily Easter-September daily
11am-5pm, October-Easter
Saturday-Sunday 11am-4pm.

Sturminster Newton
Mill & Museum
Bath Road
Open: April-September Saturday-
Monday & Thursday 11am-5pm.

Wimborne Minster
Deans Court Gardens
In the centre of Wimborne Minster
Open: April-September last Sunday
in the month; Bank Holiday
Sunday & Mondays 2-6pm and
certain other days, details from
Wimborne Information Centre
(☎ 01202 886116).

Kingston Lacy House & Garden (NT)
☎ 01202 883402
Open: April-October Saturday-
Wednesday; house: 12 noon-
5.30pm; garden & park: 11.30am-
6pm or dusk if earlier.

Merley Bird Gardens
Merley
☎ 01202 883790
Open daily all year 10.30am-
6.30pm or dusk if earlier.

Merley House & Model Museum
Merley
☎ 01202 886533
Open: Easter-October Saturday-
Thursday and Bank Holiday
Fridays 10am-4.30m.

Model Town & Gardens
King Street, BH21 1DY
☎ 01202 881924
Open: early April-September daily
10am-5pm.

Priest's House Museum of East Dorset
Life & Garden
23-27 High Street
☎ 01202 882533
Open: April-October Monday-
Saturday 10.30am-5pm; Bank
Holiday Sundays & Sundays June-
September 2-5pm.

Dorset Heavy Horse Centre
Verwood BH21 5RJ
☎ 01202 824040
Open: Easter-October daily 10am-
5pm, November-Easter Tuesday-
Sunday 11am-4pm.

Tourist Information Centres

Blandford Forum
☎ 01258 427652

Bournemouth
☎ 01202 789789

Christchurch
☎ 01202 471780

Poole
☎ 01202 673322

Shaftesbury
☎ 01747 3514

Wimborne Minster
☎ 01202 886116

South Dorset

7

In this chapter there are three main centres from which excursions and outings can be made. Dorchester is the county town of Dorset, to the south is Weymouth, and Wareham is east. Swanage is a little further east, rather cut off from the rest by the Purbeck Hills, with its approaches guarded by the imposing remains of Corfe Castle.

Choosing Dorchester as a centre will allow exploration northwards along the A352. **Minterne**, 2 miles north of Cerne Abbas, is the beautiful setting for a large garden in a lovely valley beside the River Cerne. The gardens have many varieties of Himalayan and Chinese rhododendrons and Japanese cherry trees. Further north, by about half a mile, is a minor road left going west up to Telegraph Hill. Nearby is a picnic site and from the highest point of the hill a bridleway goes south-east along East Hill. It descends, swinging west, to join another track. Turn right and walk up the combe to enter the wood. The road is beyond the woods, and a turn right returns to the starting point.

Cerne Abbas village lies quietly just off the A352. Ethelmaer, Earl of Cornwall, founded the original abbey in AD987. The usual growth went with the abbey and what amounted to a small town grew up round it, holding an important place in the lives of the surrounding community.

Quite apart from the fourteen public houses there was a magistrate's court, a malt house and a grain market. Industry included a tannery, as well as the making of gloves, harness and boots. Queen Victoria had a pair of button boots made here.

When the last stagecoach passed through Cerne Abbas and the railways never came — they used the next valley instead — the township and its population declined. Now it is a neat and tidy tourist attraction without being vulgar.

❋ Perhaps the virility of the Cerne Abbas Giant prevents an entire decline. The Giant has caused comment, speculation, and no doubt shock, among many people. He is ancient, but whether Roman or older is uncertain. Folklore regards him as a fertility symbol, so he is possibly older than a representation of Hercules dating from AD191 as has been suggested. Another authority suggests that the Romans merely added the club. A prominent safari park owner and a member of the aristocracy is reputedly proud of siring a daughter thanks to the aid of the Giant. Folklore decrees that women wanting to be sure of bearing children should sit, or sleep, on the Giant's phallus.

The Giant is now fenced off to prevent damage from too many trampling feet, but in any event by far the best view is from the lay-by on the A352, just north of the village, where there is also an information board.

Legend tells of a secret passage from the abbey up to Cat and Chapel Hill. Cat and Chapel may be a corruption of St Catherine's Chapel, so perhaps the passage went between abbey and chapel.

Just over a mile south of Cerne Abbas is **Nether Cerne**, a tiny hamlet with a manor house and a couple of cottages. The late thirteenth-century church of All Saints is cared for by the Redundant Churches Fund.

Less than a mile south is **Godmanstone**. Its claim to fame is that its pub is the smallest in England. The story is that Charles II stopped by a smithy and asked for a drink. The blacksmith said he must refuse as he had no licence, so Charles granted him a licence on the spot and 'The Smith's Arms' was instantly created.

Just over a mile north of Dorchester is **Charminster** and Wolfeton
House, which was formerly a moated manor dating from the fourteenth century. There is a medieval gatehouse and the main house
has a fine staircase and Jacobean oak carvings, although only what
was the impressive south-west corner of the house remains. In 1506
Phillip, King of Castile, was a guest here. Travelling from the
Netherlands with his wife their ship was driven into Weymouth by
a storm. The great house of the district was Wolfeton so it was only
natural that this was where they were taken.

Dorchester requires a few days to itself. The Dorset County
Museum has collections showing Dorset's natural history, prehis-
tory and geology. There is also the reconstructed study of Thomas
Hardy, and the museum contains the largest collection of poems,
manuscripts and letters written by him.

Also in the town is the Keep Military Museum. Hitler's desk is on
display, along with a diorama of the Battle of Plassey. Other items of
interest tell the story of the Queen's Own Dorset Yeomanry, the
Militia Volunteers and the Dorset Regiment. There are displays of
uniforms, firearms and medals dating back through history.

Dorchester Old Crown Court is open to the public; it was the
scene of the trial of the Tolpuddle Martyrs. They were sentenced
here for the 'crime' of forming a Friendly Society, a forerunner of a
trades union. Each was sentenced to 7 years transportation.

In Icen Way is the Dinosaur Museum, with fossils, skeletons and
lifesize reconstructions. There are also audio-visual presentations.

In High West Street is a spectacular exhibition of facsimilies of
Tutankhamen's treasures, including the famous golden mask.

Just south is the gigantic Stone Age hillfort of **Maiden Castle**, the
finest in Britain. In 2,000BC there was a Stone Age village on the site,
later there was an Iron Age village, while the Romans, commanded
by Vespasian, captured the fort about AD44. The discovery in 1937
of a war cemetery with some forty bodies in it disclosed one with a
Roman arrowhead embedded in the spine. The Romans laid out
Dorchester (*Durnovaria*) and the Roman walls determined the lines
of the Walks, the lovely tree lined avenues. These Walks were laid
out at the time of Queen Anne when the walls were levelled and the
trees planted.

Roman Dorchester covered about 85 acres and recent excavations
have discovered remains, but much of the Roman town must lie
under the modern town. Many finds are on display in the museum.
The Romans found an ancient stone circle and transformed it into
the amphitheatre now known as Maumbury Rings (near the traffic

Maiden Castle hillfort, near Dorchester

lights on the Weymouth road). In medieval England the area was used for jousts, tournaments and revels on May Day. In the Civil War the Parliamentary forces garrisoned it as a fort and lowered the southern bank so that their guns could command the Weymouth road. One of the last events to take place here was the execution of Mary Channing. For poisoning her husband she was strangled and then burned, before an audience of 10,000 people.

Dorchester is a pleasant place to stroll around. By the river there is a charming walk, while there are pleasant gardens close to playing fields and the avenues measure over a mile. A walk round the

town, following the town trail, will be most rewarding. A bronze statue of William Barnes, parson and poet, stands by St Peter's Church. Another, of Thomas Hardy, stands at the junction of High West Street and The Grove.

St Peter's Church is in the centre of the town. It is mainly fifteenth century with a 28m (90ft) tower, and there are some fine features, graceful arcades on each side of the nave, a wagon roof, panelled arches and Jacobean pulpit.

The Church of Holy Trinity is Victorian but it is the fifth church to be built on the site. All Saints is in the middle of the town and the tall nineteenth-century spire rises above the surrounding rooftops.

Fordington St George Church has splendid views over the surrounding countryside. One of the treasures of the church is a Roman carved stone, one of the earliest known in Britain. The inscription is to the memory of a Roman citizen by his wife and children. In the churchyard lie German soldiers, imprisoned here during World War I, guarded by an imposing sculpture of a kneeling German soldier.

South-west, on quiet minor roads, there is the oddly shaped **Hardy Monument**, which has been likened to a factory chimney! It was erected, not to Dorset's man of letters, but to Thomas Masterman Hardy, scholar of Milton Abbas school and later Lord Nelson's flag captain, in whose arms Lord Nelson died. The monument is a 22m (70ft) tall octagonal tower, 230m (700ft) up on Black Down, and it can be seen by passing ships. This fact would no doubt have pleased the admiral, as he became in the later stages of his naval career. He was born a little further west at Kingston Russell House. Black Down was the site of a beacon, one of the chain set up in 1804 to spread the alarm should the French invade. There are splendid views all round from the top of the Down, although the steps up the momument are now closed. Weymouth, Portland, Chesil Beach and Abbotsbury can all be seen.

A walk of about 4 miles may be made from here. East from the momument, just below the hill, a bridleway goes south-east to Bronkham Hill. The crest of the ridge is littered with tumuli stretching right along to Corton Down. Here turn south towards the sea. Turn right along the road and soon right again on another bridleway which climbs back up to the starting point.

Portesham is an interesting little village. Like most villages it has an increasing number of modern houses and bungalows on the outskirts, but there are many old cottages of mellow grey stone and two hostelries catering for visitors. At the top of the village is a delightful pool fed by a spring. Too grand to be a mere duck pond it has a nesting box set in the middle, designed to be a secure nesting place for ducks or moorhens. A stream chuckles its way down the main road past the fifteenth-century church. Admiral Hardy lived here as a boy, and again later in his life. He called the village his 'beloved Possum', possibly a corruption of the local dialect.

Two miles west along the B3157 is Abbotsbury, while further along this road to West Bay there is some very dramatic scenery. At **Abbotsbury** are the remains of a Benedictine abbey with part of the gatehouse and dovecote. Nearby is the thatched tithe barn, one of

the largest in England, which now houses a collection of agricultural and rural bygones. One of the Danes who were raiding in force
during the early part of the eleventh century was Cnut (or Canute).
Cnut besieged London and in 1017 was recognised as King of
England. Along with many of his followers, he became a Christian.
One of these followers, Urk, with his wife, Thola, was given land at
Abbotsbury and founded the abbey. It survived for 500 years until
the dissolution when the buildings were demolished. Only part of
the nave and the gatehouse now remain.

In the village are a number of workshops making and selling
quality arts and crafts.

On a hill just south, and surrounded by lynchets (medieval culti-
vation terraces) is St Catherine's Chapel. Built in the fourteenth
century its dimensions are only 15 x 5m (45 x 15ft). The walls are
over a metre (3ft) thick, as it was built to stand up to the gales
blowing in from Lyme Bay.

One mile south of Abbotsbury is the Swannery, with over six
hundred free flying swans, along with many other species, some
permanent visitors, others seasonal. The swannery, at the westward
end of the Fleet, a lagoon behind Chesil Beach, is thought to have
been started by the Abbots of Abbotsbury in Saxon times. The
cygnets hatch from the end of May to the end of June, but there is
something of interest throughout the year.

The Sub-Tropical Gardens, in a very sheltered 20-acre woodland
valley to the west of the village, contain over 7,000 varieties of rare
and exotic sub-tropical plants, trees and shrubs.

Chesil is an Old English word for shingle and **Chesil Beach** is a 10-
mile long bank of pebbles with the width varying from 180 to 900m
(200-1,000yd). It is a natural formation with a reputation for dangerous currents, shipwrecks and a variety of cast up objects. It is unique
in Europe and was supposedly cast up in one night by a great storm.
In the old days smugglers claimed to be able to locate their landfall
by the size of the pebbles, which are graded in size along the bank.

A very tough walk of 10 miles is all the way along the pebbles
from Abbotsbury to Portland. In summer it is possible to return by
bus, which runs along the B3157 to Bridport.

Inland is Kingston Russell stone circle, a pleasant round trip walk
of just under 2 miles from the minor road, although the stone circle
itself is rather undramatic. Due north and just in the next field are
some hut circles which remain as mounds visible on the ground.
There must have been a great deal of activity on these Downs many
years ago for the whole area is rich in tumuli and standing stones.

South of Dorchester lie Weymouth and Portland. **Weymouth** is a seaside holiday resort and has entertainments of all kinds to offer the visitor. There are facilities for tennis, bowls, golf, riding, yachting and fishing, either coarse on Radipole Lake, which feeds into the harbour, or sea fishing can be arranged. Bathing is possible from the firm sands of the bay or in an indoor heated pool.

Weymouth has been a sea port since Roman times, the harbour entrance is well sheltered and vessels may enter or leave at any time regardless of the state of tide, unless they are over 5m (15ft) draught. Now cross-Channel ferries operate from the port to the Channel Islands and Cherbourg.

There is a town trail which goes through Weymouth on both sides of the harbour. It passes the Tudor House in Trinity Street, which the Weymouth Civic Society has restored and opened to the public. This seventeenth-century house is furnished with objects of the period. Further along the trail is the Back Dog Inn in St Mary Street, probably the oldest tavern in the town. Blockhouse Lane is named after the ancient fortifications which once stood nearby. At nearby Preston are the foundations of a small Romano-Celtic temple.

At Brewers Quay in Hope Square a Victorian brewery has been

Abbotsbury

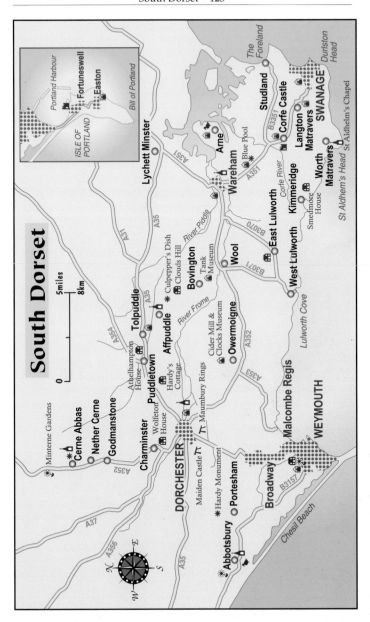

converted to include a shopping village, craft centre, cafés, restaurants and bars as well as the Weymouth Museum and Timewalk, where 'a secret passage beckons you through a magical and unforgettable journey in time'.

Nothe Gardens, south across the harbour from the town centre, are a delight to stroll or sit in and watch the harbour activity. Sandsfoot Castle, overlooking the harbour mouth, was built by Henry VIII in 1539. Although now only a ruin it was at one time described as a 'right goodlie fortress'. Dominating the mouth of the Old Harbour is the Victorian Nothe Fort, with panoramic views from its ramparts. The seventy rooms of the fort have been restored with guns, weapons and equipment to depict garrison life of the Victorian and World War II soldiers stationed here.

Weymouth is almost always associated with Portland. That is because the Isle of Portland is linked to the mainland at Weymouth by a tenuous thread of road which must cross Ferry Bridge. The land link is by way of Chesil Beach, which of course carried no road. **Portland** is one of Britain's natural wonders, a huge mound of stone projecting into the Channel and culminating in the famous Portland Bill with its lighthouse. Stone has been quarried at Portland only fairly recently but there is evidence of Roman use; to them it was probably a secure fortress. Verne Citadel, built by convict labour in the 1860s as a fortress at a time when the government was alarmed at the possibility of a French invasion, is now a Borstal Training Centre. Halfway down the east coast is the ruined twelfth-century Rufus Castle. A different sort of castle, built in 1800 by John Penn, the Governor of Portland, is Pennsylvania Castle, now an hotel.

Inigo Jones was impressed by Portland stone and used it for the banqueting hall of Whitehall Palace. Later Wren used it for St Paul's. As much as 100,000 tons were quarried in one year as the fashion for Portland stone grew.

No one could call Portland beautiful, but it is interesting. A fine view of Chesil Beach can be seen from the summit, and just east is Portland Harbour enclosing over 2,000 acres. The breakwaters took over twenty years to build. It was the home base of the Channel Fleet, but the future of the port is uncertain as it is to be sold when the Navy leave.

In July the spectacular Navy Days, a two day event, draw thousands of visitors. Portland Castle is now part of the dockyard, but it was built by Henry VIII and was one of the last strongholds to surrender to Cromwell. There are displays of cannon and reproductian Elizabethan armour. Portland Museum is housed in two cottages which were given by Dr Marie Stopes. The museum records the history of Portland, the stone industry, the prison service, shipwrecks, smuggling and has a comprehensive fossil collection. Down at the southern tip is a car park, a café and Portland Bill lighthouse. There is a footpath going most of the way round the island, giving a walk of about 8 miles.

Moving east, the A353 joins the A352 Dorchester to Weymouth road, and a couple of miles east of the junction at **Owermoigne** is the unusual combination of the Mill House Cider Museum and the Dorset Collection of Clocks. At the cider museum you can see antique apple presses and other equipment restored to working condition, while the clock collection includes about fifty longcase ('grandfather') clocks made in the county.

North of the A352 the A35 goes from Dorchester to Poole and Bournemouth. To the south of the A35 and down to the coast there is plenty to do and to see. From the A35 just east of Dorchester a small diversion south leads to **Kingston Maurward** with 35 acres of gardens and a farm animal park.

Nearby is **Higher Bockhampton** and Thomas Hardy's cottage where the novelist and poet was born in 1840. The cottage itself was built by Hardy's grandfather and is in almost original condition. It is a National Trust property and viewing is by written appointment with the tenant, but the garden is open every day. It is approached by a 10-minute walk through the woods. Here it was that Hardy wrote *Far from The Madding Crowd* and *Under the Greenwood Tree.*

Hardy's cottage is on the edge of Puddletown Forest. On the other side of the forest, and approached from **Puddletown**, is a picnic site and 2-mile forest trail to a good viewpoint over the forest to the Purbeck Hills. The trail starts from the picnic site near Beacon Corner at the top of White Hill.

Half a mile east of Puddletown is Athelhampton, a medieval house which has been a family home for over eight hundred years and is one of the finest examples of fifteenth-century domestic architecture in the country. The heraldic glass shows the coats of arms of the families connected with the house, and there is a fine collection of furniture on display. There are large formal gardens balanced by woodland and riverside scenes. The house was built by Sir William Martyn who died in 1503. He was Lord Mayor of London in 1493 at about the time the house building was started. Martyns held the house and estate until 1595 when Nicholas Martyn died, leaving four daughters but no son to inherit.

Before leaving Puddletown stop in the Square to look at the row

Looking ahead to St Oswald's Bay and Durdle Door

Lulworth Crumple folded rock strata

of nineteenth-century thatched cottages, a Tudor cottage built in 1573 and the brick-built vicarage, dated 1722. The last Roman Catholic Archbishop of Canterbury, Cardinal Pole, was vicar of St Mary's Church for three years. Nicholas Martyn is remembered in the church and there are earlier brasses. There is also a fine stone memorial of a knight and his lady dated about 1300.

Tolpuddle lies another 2 miles east. Who has not heard of the Tolpuddle Martyrs? Six farm labourers met one morning in 1831 and vowed to form a union to ask for an increase, to ten shillings (fifty pence) a week from the seven shillings (thirty-five pence) wages they then received. They swore an oath of secrecy and for this 'crime' they were sentenced in 1834 to seven years transportation. The outcry at this savage sentence on six hardworking men, two of whom were local lay preachers, forced the government to grant them pardon. However, it took a long time for the pardon to reach Australia, and even then no trouble was taken to find the men. One of them, James Hammett, who was working on a lonely sheep station, read about his pardon 4 years later when he picked up an old newspaper! This was the first he knew, and but for this chance action he may well have served out his full sentence.

James Hammett is buried in the local churchyard. In 1934 the Trades Union Congress built a row of six cottages and it is now a museum of the events of 1834. The Martyrs' Tree, where the men met, is also a memorial, as is a plaque on a cottage which was the home of one of the martyrs. A gate at the Wesleyan Chapel commemorates the events that shook the world at the time.

South on the minor road from Tolpuddle is **Affpuddle**, a lovely village on the B3390. The church of St Laurence has a fine tower of grey stone and flint. It is mainly fifteenth century with a thirteenth-century chancel. In the church is a monument bearing the arms of the Lawrence family. The arms, which are quartered with stars and stripes, are said to have been the inspiration for the flag of the United States of America. George Washington's mother was a Lawrence.

Affpuddle Heath lies south of Affpuddle — Hardy used it as Egdon Heath in his novels. At Affpuddle Cross, a mile south of the village and on the east side of the road, is a picnic site set in pine forest. Three-quarters of a mile east on the minor road is another picnic site, set on heathland and close to Culpepper's Dish which is believed to be the largest natural 'swallet' hole in Europe. This is a large circular pit with attendant smaller ones. They were thought for a long time to have been ancient dwellings. However they are of natural formation and caused by softer parts of the natural chalk subsiding, possibly when sand moved below the surface.

A mile south-east is Clouds Hill and the cottage of T. E. Lawrence (Lawrence of Arabia). He bought the small cottage after renting it for a time when he was serving in the Tank Corps at Bovington. When he left the services in 1935 he lived at the cottage for a short time before his fatal motorcycle accident.

South-east again by about a mile is **Bovington Camp**, an unlovely typical military base, with the heath round about scarred by erosive tracks, although afforestation is being used to repair the damage. For military enthusiasts Bovington is a must, as it is the home of the Royal Armoured Corps Tank Museum. What began as a collection of twenty-six British and French tanks in 1923 has now grown to over 150 tracked and wheeled vehicles. Apart from Britain nine other Commonwealth and foreign nations are represented. The museum shows the development of the armoured vehicle together with armaments, ammunition and engines. There are photographs, models, uniforms and personal mementos. All the regiments have their own regimental museums, but often space prevents large displays, so the Tank Museum houses the armoured vehicles as the general museum of the Royal Armoured Corps.

South again is **Wool**, where there is a sixteenth-century bridge across the River Frome. Woolbridge Manor, now an hotel, was built in the seventeenth century, and was once the home of the real-life Turbervilles. This was the house where Hardy sent Tess of the D'Urbervilles for her honeymoon. The B3071 south from Wool goes to West Lulworth and on to Lulworth Cove. Both are very busy in the holiday season, but **West Lulworth** has some interesting cottages. **Lulworth Cove** appears in nearly every geography textbook as a classic example of a ridge of hard rock through which the sea has broken to form a nearly circular bay in the softer rock beheind. To the east are army ranges where tanks test their guns, so the paths are often closed, but to the west is a cliff-top path to the rock arch known as Durdle Door and on to Ringstead Bay, 5 miles away. Here turn inland and join a bridleway back over the Beacons to Daggers Gate and down the road back to the church at West Lulworth.

At **East Lulworth** is Lulworth Castle, which was built in the early seventeenth century as a romantic hunting lodge and changed into a fashionable country house in the eighteenth century. Although gutted by fire in 1929 the exterior is being restored and the parts that may be visited include a viewing area at the top of the tower.

Kimmeridge bay is reached by a toll road down to a grass car

Corfe Castle

park. The great black slabs of rock in place of a beach could be a disappointment to some, but the place is a favourite with divers.

✳ Clavel Tower, a folly on the east cliff, was built about 1820 by the Rev John Richards, who inherited the nearby Smedmore House. The tower is unsafe and fenced off. On the other side of the bay, and well concealed, is a 'nodding donkey' oil well. Oil has been extracted here since 1961 at a rate of 100,000 gallons a week. The machinery is painted green to blend in with the background, which it does very well.

⌂ **Smedmore House** was built by Sir William Clavel in 1632; the original parts of the house are still visible, but the west front and

Cliffs near Old Harry Rocks

Moorings alongside the River Frome at Wareham

entrance are eighteenth century. Inside are examples of fine eighteenth-century plasterwork and an oak staircase. The house is only open on Wednesdays in the summer, but it is worth a visit. Much original furniture, collections of Dresden china and dolls, and the gardens make up the interest at this fine old house.

Inland are the Purbeck Hills and the Isle of Purbeck. Why Isle? Well, consider the geography. The Purbeck Hills reach from Ballard Down, to the north of Swanage, through Corfe Castle almost to Lulworth. East Lulworth is relatively low lying, as a break in the cliff occurs at Arish Mell. North is Luckford Lake, a small stream feeding into the River Frome, which in turn runs into Poole Harbour. In the old days the low lying land would have been very boggy and difficult to cross in winter, hence the 'island' of Purbeck.

The Purbeck Hills are cut at **Corfe Castle**, which guarded the gap. The castle has had a long and violent history. Elfrida, widow of King Edgar, had a hunting lodge at Corfe in 978. King Edgar's son Edward was killed at the gates as he called at his step-mother's house. She later took holy vows and retreated to Wherwell Priory. Her son Ethelred came to the throne, possibly too young, and earned the soubriquet 'The Unready'.

After the Norman Conquest, Corfe became a 'royal' castle, begun in 1080. Many royal prisoners were held here. One dungeon was only entered by a trapdoor in the roof; presumably no-one left it alive! Twenty-two French knights were left to starve here by King John. Eleanor of Brittany was a prisoner, as was King Edward II.

The castle was held for the crown during the Civil War by Lady Bankes, wife of Sir John. Two sieges were held off and the castle was only taken by treachery. In 1646 Parliament voted to have the castle destroyed. Though blasted and mined the castle did not entirely fall and it is still an impressive and awe inspiring sight. The leaning towers and large blocks of fallen stone give the impression that the castle is falling down, whereas in fact the remains seen today are the result of Parliamentarian engineers and not the ravages of time.

The village of Corfe Castle nestling at the foot of the fortress is unspoilt and still has the air of a medieval village. Behind the church there is a small local museum in the town hall, England's smallest.

From Corfe Castle there is a ridge walk in each direction. East to Ballard Point is 6 miles, with splendid views on a clear day over Poole Harbour. West to Grange Arch, a Victorian 'folly', is just under 3 miles. Down the road and over the fields is Kimeridge Bay, with a cliff walk back to Swanage for the really energetic.

The Swanage Railway runs steam trains from Norden, near Corfe

Castle to Swanage along a line that was closed in 1972, but has been restored by a dedicated band of volunteers.

Just west of Swanage is **Langton Matravers** where the Coach House Museum tells the story of the Purbeck stone industry, including a reconstruction of an underground stone quarry. At the Putlake Adventure Farm children can meet the friendly farm animals.

Swanage is a small seaside resort with a good beach that is very busy in the summer months, a pier from which it is possible to fish, and a harbour from which to organise a sea fishing trip. The Great Globe, carved from a single piece of Portland stone, shows all the countries of the world as they were in Victorian times. In the centre of Swanage, by the parish church an historic tithe barn has been converted into a local museum, arts, crafts and exhibition centre.

While in the area take the chance to see the stone quarries at **Worth Matravers.** These great quarries were in production until the mid-1940s. South from Worth Matravers is the twelfth-century St Aldhelm's Chapel. Only 8m (25ft) square, it stands on the most southerly point of the Isle of Purbeck, St Aldhelm's Head. Durlston Head, south of Swanage, has a country park with access to the cliff walks and views of the lighthouse at Avil Point. Durlston Castle was built in 1890 as a restaurant, which it still is. It was built by a stone merchant named George Burt, who installed the first pumped water supply at Swanage, and also brought various items of London masonry to enhance the town.

On the northern side of the Purbeck Hills from Swanage lies **Studland Bay**. This mile-long stretch of well sheltered beach is a great favourite in the summer. Perhaps the most rewarding way to visit Studland is over Ballard Down, or by way of the longer Dorset Coast Path along the cliff edge, passing the Old Harry Rocks. The bridleway over Ballard Down leads directly down to the Anglo-Saxon church which stands on the site of an earlier church which the Danes destroyed in the ninth century. That church had been built about the seventh century on the site of an even earlier building, possibly a pre-Christian temple.

Inland, Studland Heath leads on to Newton, Rempstone, Wytch, Middlebere, Slepe and Arne Heaths, all within some 6 or 7 miles and all on the shores of Poole Harbour. The last one, Arne, has a nature trail and bird sanctuary, and the central portion is criss-crossed by pathways. In the village of **Arne** you can relive the nostalgia of childhood at the Purbeck Toy and Musical Box Museum.

On the other side of the A351 is **Blue Pool**. This lovely place came into being because of the demand for clay, which as long ago as

1650, was in heavy demand, for making tobacco pipes and pottery. Clay was transported by sea and canal to the famous potteries of Wedgwood and Minton. The area has recovered and the woods and heath around the pool are now a haven of peace and quiet. There is a picnic area, a tea house and a gift shop. The museum shows the growth of the clay mining industry, with displays of clay tobacco pipes, fine examples of ceramics and Chinese porcelain salvaged from a Dutch ship wrecked in the South China Seas.

Wareham is an ancient town and was once an important sea port. Its fortified site is between the Rivers Frome and Piddle or Trent. The town was founded in 705 by the first Bishop of Sherborne. Its varied history includes fortification by the Romans and sacking by the sea-roving Danes. There are three ancient churches, including the small St Martins on the Wall, which has an effigy of Lawrence of Arabia.

The Wareham Museum on East Street has displays of local history and a collection of photographs and ephemera of Lawrence of Arabia. Part of the old town walls can still be seen and there are some old buildings, although much of the town was destroyed by fire in the late eighteenth century and the majority of buildings date from that period. Wareham now has an east-west bypass saving the town centre from the worst congestion.

No visit to Wareham would be complete without visiting Wareham Forest. There is a picnic site at Gore Heath, on the B3075 2 miles north, and another at Coldharbour 2 miles north-west on a minor road. At the Coldharbour site there is a nature trail of 1½ miles which includes Morden Bog Nature Reserve and a small arboretum. The Wessex Way passes through the forest. This walk joins up the Ridgeway at Avebury in Wiltshire to Swanage. It enters Dorset from Wiltshire over Bokerley Dyke (see Chapter 6) so anyone wanting a good long walk could follow this route.

Additional Information

Accommodation

£££ = expensive
££ = moderate
£ = inexpensive
EM = evening meal available

Abbotsbury

*Millmead Country Hotel
& Restaurant* (£££, EM)
Goose Hill, Portesham, DT3 4HE
☎ 01305 871432

Cerne Abbas

Mr & Mrs Munn (££)
The Singing Kettle, 7 Long Street,
DT2 7JF
☎ 01300 341349
Food available nearby.

Dorchester

Wessex Royale Hotel (££, EM)
32 High Street West, DT1 1UP
☎ 01305 262660

Kimmeridge

Mrs A. Hole (££, EM)
Kimmeridge Farmhouse, BH20 5NU
☎ 01929 480990

Martinstown

Jane Rootham (£, EM)
The Old Post Office, DT2 9LF
☎ 01305 889252

Swanage

Chines Hotel (£, EM)
9 Burlington Road, BH19 1LR
☎ 01929 422457

Winterbourne Abbas

Mr & Mrs Deller (££, EM)
Churchview Guest House, DT2 9LS
☎ 01305 889296

Lulworth Cove

Cromwell House Hotel (£, EM)
West Lulworth, BH20 5RJ
☎ 01929 400253

Places to Visit

Abbotsbury

Abbotsbury Sub-Tropical Gardens
☎ 01305 871387
Open: daily March-October 10am-
6pm, November-February 10am-
4pm. Last entry 1 hour before
closing. Closed 25-26 December, 1
January.

Abbotsbury Swannery
☎ 01305 871684
Open March-October daily 10am-
6pm. Last entry 5pm.

Tithe Barn Country Museum
☎ 01305 871817
Open: March-October daily from 10am.

Cerne Abbas

Minterne Gardens
Minterne Magna
☎ 0130 341370
Open: April-October daily 10am-7pm.

Corfe Castle

Corfe Castle (NT)
Ruins open: daily, March-October
10am-5.30pm; November-February
12 noon-3.30pm. Closed 25-26
December.

Town Hall & Museum
West Street
Open: April-October, 9am-5pm.
Admission free.

Dorchester

Dinosaur Museum
Icen Way
☎ 01305 269880
Open: daily 9.30am-5.30pm

Dorset County Museum
High Street West
☎ 01305 262735
Open: Monday-Saturday 10am-5pm;
Sunday 10am-5pm July & August.

Hardy's Cottage (NT)
Higher Bockhampton, DT2 8QT
Garden open: April-October,
Friday-Wednesday 11am-6pm.
Cottage open by written appointment only.

The Keep Military Museum
The Keep, Bridport Road, DT1 1RN
☎ 01305 264066
Open: Monday to Saturday 9.30am-
5pm, Saturday 9.30am-1pm, 2-5pm.

Kingston Maurward Gardens
☎ 01305 264 738
Open: mid-April to mid-October
daily 10am-5pm.

Old Crown Court & Cells
Old Shire Hall, Stratton House,
High St West, DT1 1UZ
☎ 01305 252241
Open: Monday- Friday 10am-12
noon, 2-4pm. Tours of the cells late
July-August Monday- Friday 2.15-
4.15pm. Closed Bank Holidays.

Tutankhamen Exhibition
High Street West
☎ 01305 269571
Open: daily 9.30am-5.30pm.

Wolfeton House
Charminster
☎ 01305 263500
Open: May-September, Tuesday,
Thursday and Bank Holidays 2-6pm.

East Lulworth
Lulworth Castle
☎ 01929 400510
Open: daily April-October 10am-
6pm, November-December 10am-
4pm.

Kimmeridge
Smedmore House
☎ 01929 480717
Open: June to mid-September
Wednesday 2.15-5.30pm. Teas in
the village a mile away.

Owermoigne
Mill House Cider Museum
Dorset Collection of Clocks
☎ 01305 852220
Open: daily 9am-5pm. Closed 25-
28 December, 1 January.

Portland
Portland Bill Lighthouse
Open: Monday-Saturday 1pm to 1
hour before sunset, unless foggy.

Portland Castle
☎ 01305 820539
Open: daily April-September
10am-6pm, October 10am-4pm.

*Portland Museum & Shipwreck
   Exhibition*
217 Wakeham
☎ 01305 821804
Open: Easter-October daily,
November-Easter Friday-Tuesday
10.30am-1pm, 1.30-5pm.

Puddletown
Athelhampton
☎ 01305 848363
Open: April-October, Tuesday-
Thursday, Sunday and Bank
Holidays, also Monday and Friday
in August, 12 noon-5pm.

Swanage
Coach House Museum
Langton Matravers
☎ 01929 423168/423866/439372
Open: April-October Monday-
Saturday 10am-12 noon, 2-4pm.

Putlake Adventure Farm
Langton Matravers
☎ 01929 423751/422917
Open: Easter-October Sunday-
Friday 11am-6pm.

Swanage Railway
Station House, Swanage BH19 1HB
☎ 01929 425800
Regular steam trains from Swanage

to Corfe Castle mid-April to September. Limited service at other periods. Check timetables.

Tithe Barn
Church Hill
☎ 01929 424566
Open: summer Monday-Saturday 10.30am-12.30pm, 2.30-4.30pm, 7.30-9.30pm; Sunday 2.30-4.30pm.

Tolpuddle
Tolpuddle Martyrs Museum
TUC Memorial Cottages
☎ 01305 848237
Open: April-October Tuesday-Saturday 10am-5.30pm, Sunday 11-5.30pm, Bank Holidays 10am-5.30pm. Winter closes 1 hour earlier. Closed 25 December- 1 January. Admission free.

Wareham
Blue Pool
Furzebrook
☎ 01929 551408
Grounds open: March-November from 9.30am.
Museum open: Easter-early October.

Clouds Hill (NT)
Turnerspuddle
☎ 01985 847777
Open: April-October, Wednesday-Friday, Sunday and Bank Holiday Monday 2-5pm or dusk if earlier.

Purbeck Toy & Musical Box Museum
Arne
☎ 01929 552018
Open: Tuesday-Friday & Sunday April-June, September 1.30-5pm; July-August 10.30am-5.30pm. Also Bank Holiday Mondays & daily in August.

Tank Museum
Bovington Camp, BH20 6JG
☎ 01929 405105
Open: daily 10am-5pm.

Wareham Museum
East Street
☎ 01929 553448
Open: Easter to mid-October Monday-Saturday 10am-1pm, 2-5pm.

Weymouth
Brewers Quay Museum
Hope Square, Old Harbour
☎ 01305 777622
Open: daily 9.30am-5.30pm (till 9.30pm in school summer holidays). Closed 25-26 December.

Nothe Fort
Barrack Road
☎ 01305 787243
Open: May-September daily 10.30am-5.30pm; winter Sunday & Bank Holidays 2-4pm.

Tudor House
3 Trinity Street
☎ 01305 782925/788168
Open: June-September Tuesday-Friday 11am-3.45pm, October-May 1st Sunday in month 2-4pm.

Tourist Information Centres

Dorchester
Acland Road
☎ 01305 267992

Swanage
Shore Road, BH19 1LB
☎ 01929 422885

Wareham
Town Hall, East Street, BH20 4NN
☎ 019295 552740

Weymouth
The Esplanade
☎ 01305 785747
0800 765223 (accommodation)

Between the Thames & Wansdyke

8

The very best of rural England and still so little known. Yet communication could not be better. The M4 motorway slices off the top of Wiltshire, almost alongside the London to Bristol main railway line with express trains stopping at Swindon. Another main route the A303 trunk road crosses Wessex, entering near Amesbury and leaving near Chard. The A30 crosses the area from Salisbury to Shaftesbury and on to Sherborne.

Starting at Swindon, take the B4507 to **Wanborough**. This was a very important junction of Roman roads, where a road off Ermine Street went down to Mildenhall and Winchester. Once known as the valley of Wessex, it was an important vantage point in Saxon times and the site of two battles, one in 715, when there was a long conflict between the forces of Mercia and Wessex. The church is interesting, having a stone spire dating from the fourteenth century and a

above: Aldbourne

Wanborough

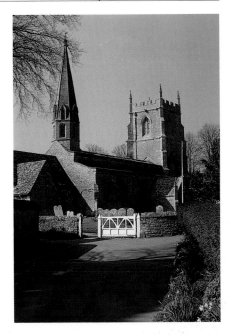

pinnacled tower at the west end dating from the fifteenth century.
Inside the north porch is a notice board requesting all females to
remove their pattens (raised shoes for walking through mud) on
entering the church.

Leave by the B4507 towards Wantage and it is not far to **Hinton
Parva**, a tiny hamlet mostly to the north of the road. The church is
part Norman and part Perpendicular.

There are views to the north across the Thames Valley from along
the road, which soon arrives at **Bishopstone**; the church is Perpendicular but the font is Norman. There is some medieval glass and a
clock which was made locally in the seventeenth century. To the
south of the road is a group of cottages round a pond and a narrow
path leads round this idyllic 'time capsule'.

The county border is only half a mile away. Returning to Hinton
Parva a narrow lane leads south for a mile to the Shepherd's Rest
public house. A left turn rejoins the Roman Road (Ermine Street)
going south-east to **Baydon**, where Sir Isaac Newton once lived. The
church is of twelfth century origin. A right turn here leads down to
Aldbourne.

Aldbourne is a typical peaceful and proper village. It has all the ingredients — a constant unchanging population figure, continuous occupation since the Bronze age, a duck pond on the village green, a village pump and an ancient cross. There are attractive cottages of brick and thatch, including a sixteenth-century court house. The Crown Inn was a coach staging post and the ostlers' rooms and the mounting block are still there. There was a bell foundry here in the seventeenth and eighteenth centuries and the village was famous for its fairs and markets. Aldbourne Church is fifteenth century, and has, among many notable features, the tomb near the altar in which lies John Stone (1501); it is a fine piece of carving.

Aldbourne Chase is a long green trough running north-east, unfortunately carrying the A419 trunk road, towards Liddington. It was said to have been a favourite area with King John, while John of Gaunt was a frequent visitor. There was a Civil War skirmish in the chase.

Go south-east down the A419 through the hamlet of Knighton and alongside the River Kennet for the run into Chilton Foliat. Look to the south across the river; Littlecote House is a magnificent sight. But pause at **Chilton Foliat** before going on. This is an attractive village of timbered cottages and Georgian houses. The thirteenth-century church is of flint and stone and there are some interesting features.

After crossing the river a right turn leads to Littlecote House. Settlement on the site certainly goes back to Roman times. A mosaic was laid in AD360 in the Roman villa which itself dated from AD170. This mosaic was discovered in the eighteenth century but reburied by the owners to avoid publicity. It was rediscovered in 1977 and the whole villa area of about 3 acres is now uncovered.

Littlecote House itself is a splendid Tudor red brick mansion, still a family home. There was a house on the site, or a hamlet, in the thirteenth century but the present house is sixteenth with one remaining fifteenth-century section. During the Civil War, Colonel Popham was a Roundhead and he garrisoned his officers at the house. King Charles II pardoned the owner, who was also intrumental in restoring him to the throne, and dined in the house in 1663. The house is now closed to the public, except for special events.

By the river walk Littlecote is only 2 miles from Ramsbury but by road, back via Chilton Foliat, it is about 4 miles. **Ramsbury** or Ravensbury (Raven's fortified place) is a pleasant village. Most of the buildings are of red brick, pleasantly mellowed, but there are some older ones of timber and thatch; there were many more before a series of fires. The thirteenth-century church rests on the site of a Saxon church, remnants of which were discovered during restoration work in 1890. Some of these stones are on display in a corner of the church. The Bishop of Wiltshire resided in Ramsbury between AD909 and AD1058.

In the square there is a young oak tree, planted as a semi-mature tree in 1986 at the behest of a building society which had the old tree as its emblem. The original old tree was destroyed by disease but there was much local controversy as to whether it was dead. Local folklore claimed the tree to be home to the local witch, Maud Toogood.

Just west of Ramsbury the road passes the imposing gates of Ramsbury Manor, a private house, and loops round the grounds. After passing the hamlet of Axford the next point of interest is **Stitchcombe**. The hamlet proper lies to the south of the river but beside the road on the north side is Stitchcombe vineyard and shop. This is an interesting stop.

Cross the river here, turn right and then take a right fork onto a very narrow lane. This allows a view down over Black Field, quite a large area and with very little to see on the surface, but below the grass lie the remains of the Roman town or fort of *Cunetio*, where excavations have been carried out revealing an enclosure with streets laid out. Roads from there go to Wanborough, to join Ermine Street, Bath, London, Salisbury and Winchester. A Celtic vessel found here is on display in Devizes museum.

Turn right again to recross the river and reach **Mildenhall**. The old school, now a private house, is an interesting building, with four wings round a tower.

The church is of particular interest. It spans the centuries, having origins in the twelfth century with some Anglo-Saxon (in the year AD803 the abbot of Glastonbury obtained the land in 'minal' to build a new church), Norman and early English work with Perpendicular windows and late Georgian furniture. It seems to have escaped the Victorian urge to renovate, still having the Georgian high box pews and has two pulpits both with canopies and a lectern. The remnants of stained glass in the east window are claimed as some of the oldest in the country. The remainder of the window was destroyed by some of Cromwell's soldiers during the Civil War. From Mildenhall it is about a mile into Marlborough.

Marlborough's history goes back as far as any in the county. In the grounds of the college is an ancient barrow, Maerl's Barrow,

Mildenhall

Marlborough

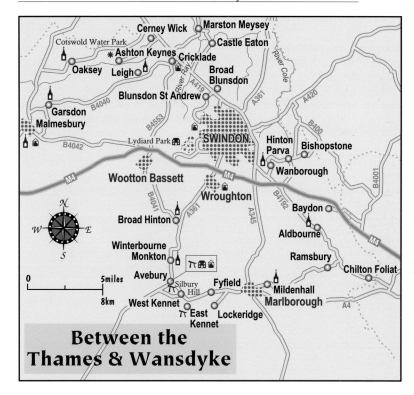

Between the Thames & Wansdyke

from which the name of the town may be derived, or it could have been 'Marle Burg', which means chalk town. Alternatively, it may have been the semi-mythical Merlin whose name has been corrupted into Marlborough. However, the Normans built a castle on Maerl's Barrow and many kings visited to hunt in the great Savernake Forest nearby. At one time coins were minted here, and Henry III summoned parliament to the castle in 1267. It was given to the Seymour family, who lived at Severnake, by Jane Seymour's son Edward VI. Samuel Pepys was entertained in the house as it became after being rebuilt by John Webb, a pupil of Inigo Jones.

Much later in 1700, the house became the Castle Inn and many famous people stayed there on route between London and Bath; it was one of the most popular inns on the way. When the railways took the trade from the coaches, the Castle Inn declined and in 1843 closed its doors. Later in 1843 it became the nucleus of Marlborough College.

The best way to enjoy Marlborough is on foot by walking along the High Street. Some say this is the finest high street in England. Despite three disastrous fires in 1653, 1679 and 1690, there is much to admire. Some of the Tudor buildings remain standing side by side with the Georgian and some modern ones. At the London end of the street is the fine town hall which stands on the site of the old market house. Behind is St Mary's Church and a little passageway leading to The Green. Here, said to be the site of a Saxon settlement, the Sheep Fairs were held until 1893 and there are some fine Georgian houses.

One of the highlights of the High Street is the White Horse Bookshop dating from 1549. There is a side passage once known as Horse Passage leading to Back Lane. There is, in fact, an excellent leaflet, *Marlborough, A Guided Walk*, which is available from the information office at St Peter's Church in the High Street, the one at the western end. The church was declared redundant some years ago and was in danger of either falling down or being demolished. Local folk got together and saved it. It is now a centre for various bodies but it has retained a side chapel for worship.

There is still a weekly market in the High Street, a reminder of the old 'Hiring Market' or 'Mop Fair'. This annual event continues to be commemorated today, in October, when Marlborough still holds its Mop Fair.

Between the A4 London Road and the A346 Andover Road the lovely **Savernake Forest** offers peace and tranquillity along the drives and paths. Though popular with visitors, the size of the forest absorbs them. One mile along the A346 from the town centre is Posterne Hill forest walk, a 2-mile trail through this ancient forest which traces its history back to pre-Norman times. Many of the fine avenues of beech trees were planted by Capability Brown over 200 years ago. Note the crenellated toll house near the A4 entrance to Grand Avenue, a 3-mile drive.

By following the A4 west, or upstream, along the River Kennet, many more wonderful mysteries unfold. At the hamlet of **Fyfield** there is a small thirteenth-century church. It has a fifteenth-century tower with gargoyles and pinnacles. North-east by half a mile is the Devil's Den, the remains of a long barrow which actually lies in Flatford Bottom. It can be a pleasant walk: from Fyfield cross the A4, with care, and go up the farm track opposite. Go up Fyfield Hill and pass the farm just over the brow then go down the enclosed track beyond the farm to a gate. Go through the gate and turn right. This is part of Fyfield Down Nature Reserve. Four hundred metres (440yd) on is a gate and a 'Reserve' sign. Devil's Den is just beyond. After viewing the stones, continue, to join a track, and so down to the A4 again. Cross on the track to Clatford, crossing the River Kennet on the way. At the second sharp left hand bend turn right. Go through a small gate into a field but maintain a westerly direction over three fields to emerge on a road which, if you turn right, will lead back to Fyfield. The Devil's Den is said to be haunted. Occasionally at midnight the Devil appears with a team of white oxen to pull the stones down.

Refreshments may be obtained at the Who'd a Thought It pub in **Lockeridge**. The village is a puzzle. Of moderate size, it has many old houses and is even mentioned in the Domesday Book. There is a school and a shop but the puzzle is that it has no church, a strange absence in such an old village. West Woods just to the south-east will provide tranquil walks, but do take a good map as the woods are not easy to negotiate without one.

Forming one boundary of West Woods but also cutting through is a part of the Wansdyke. A great linear defensive earthwork with a single bank and ditch, it has been attributed to the Saxons, against the Danes, and to the Britons, against the Saxons. The British builder was said to be the legendary Arthur. There is evidence that it was built in the sixth century.

From Lockeridge it is possible to go by way of the minor road to West Overton and on to **East Kennet** where there is a thirteenth-century church. Up on the A4 (it can be reached by footpath from the village) is The Sanctuary on Overton Hill. It consists of two concentric circles of stones and six of timber and is said to be early Bronze Age. Access is at any time.

Continuing onto the A4 and turning west the hamlet of **West Kennet** is soon reached. Less than half a mile beyond is a lay-by off the road allowing visitors to walk up to West Kennet long barrow on a plainly marked footpath. This barrow is said to be the largest of its kind in Britain. The mound is 110m (360ft) long and 2m (6$\frac{1}{2}$ft) high. In all there were forty-six burials in the tomb spanning a thousand years. Radio carbon dating suggests 2,570BC for the burials while the final closing, dated from the pottery, was 1,600BC. Old burials were, it seems, swept to one side to make room for new ones. Some of the skulls and long bones were missing. In all there were five burial chambers. Devizes museum has relics and photographs of the barrow.

The remains of a prehistoric long barrow at Devil's Den, near Fyfield

Avebury stone circle

A short distance further along the road is **Silbury Hill**. It has its own car park and viewing area, saving a dangerous walk and road crossing. Silbury is the largest prehistoric man-made hill in Europe. It covers over 5 acres and its ditch was originally much larger. It has been examined and some excavation work has been done but little of any significance has been found — it still keeps its secret. It is believed to date from 2,600BC. One theory suggests it is the burial mound of King Sil and his horse, another that there is a lifesize gold statue buried. A folktale tells of how the Devil dropped it there while on his way to Devizes. Many people have climbed to the top, and it is a good vantage point. One strange fact is that it dominates the area from both the valleys and the hill tops — if you know which way to look, Silbury Hill can be seen.

Turn back, and then left on the B4003, towards Avebury. This route leads via the stone avenue into the stone circle. The stone avenue leads from Overton Hill and The Sanctuary into Avebury. Many of the original stones are missing but their positions are now marked by cement plinths. There was once a double row of these stones which were smaller than the great circle stones, and of alternate shapes; it has been suggested they represented male and female.

At the next road junction, as **Avebury** appears ahead, a left turn will lead to a large car park with a walkway into the village. Parking is available in the village centre but it is limited. There are convenient gates at road crossings so that a walk round the great circle can be made. Imagine what the size must have been before the years took their toll. For those with a real historic interest it is a good idea to visit the local museums first. Devizes museum has lots of information on Avebury, while the local Alexander Keiller Museum, has one of the most important prehistorical collections in Britain. The earliest construction goes back to 2,500BC which is late Neolithic. There are almost a hundred stones and some of them have been calculated to weigh over 30 tons. The great travellers and historians, William Stokeley, John Aubrey and Richard Colt Hoare all worked on the site, but Alexander Keiller (who inherited the family fortune made in Dundee from marmalade) did much of the restoration work in 1934-9 when he lived in the manor house.

Avebury Manor is a fine Elizabethan house with some decorative ceilings. It was built on the site of an ancient priory which was itself founded in 1110 but at the dissolution was given to Sir John Sherington. The present house has been continuously occupied for 400 years. It is reputedly haunted. There are some fine gardens to be seen, with excellent topiary, a dovecote with doves, peacocks on the lawns and an eighteenth-century wishing well.

The village itself lies within the stone circle and has some interesting houses and old thatched cottages, many built from the great sarsen stones. A favourite way of breaking the stones in those days was supposed to be by building a fire to heat the stone, then when it was hot, causing it to cool rapidly by throwing water on it.

Another very interesting sight in the village is the exhibition of rural crafts by the Wiltshire Folk Life Society in a great thatched threshing barn. Farm tools and implements are set out in a realistic way and there are regular demonstrations of rural crafts, such as hurdle making and leatherwork, among many others.

Lying just outside the circle is the ancient church. It is a beautiful and interesting church with Saxon origins and alterations and additions going through the ages from the Normans, up through the fifteenth and sixteenth centuries, up to the oak pulpit about 1840.

The energetic can stroll the 1½ miles through **Avebury Trusloe**, where there is a good view of the private manor house, up to **Windmill Hill**. Here is the location of the earliest pottery finds in Britain, dated to about 2,570BC. Although it has been called a 'causewayed camp', it was hardly defensive, and later thinking suggests that it was for ceremonial or trade use. Perhaps ritual use as well, for there are several great barrows in the area which were in use for very many years.

Also within the village of Avebury is an antique shop, a craft shop, a store and the famous Red Lion Inn. In the forecourt of this lovely old thatched coaching inn is an old cider press. A ghost coach is said to draw up at the inn late at night. Another nearby ancient hostelry is the Waggon and Horses at **Beckhampton**. Once it was a favourite stopping place for drovers and waggoners. Nowadays it is still a very pleasant place to stop and both it and the Red Lion provide good food.

The A4361 north from Avebury leads back towards Swindon. A little over a mile north lies **Winterbourne Monkton** with a tiny but interesting church. It has an oak shingle belfry resting on wooden supports within the church. The White Horse is on Hackpen Hill where the Ridgeway runs, a lovely stretch of downland flanked by the higher ground to the east, and it is relatively modern, having been cut in the Victorian era. The next road access point to the Downs is above Wroughton, near Barbury Castle Country Park, and here Cynric, King of Wessex, with his son Caewlin, fought the Britons in 556 at the battle of Beranburgh.

Broad Hinton church is worth a visit. There is a monument to Sir Thomas Wroughton with effigies of himself and his wife and children. There is also a striking alabaster figure to Colonel Francis Glanville who died fighting for his king at Bridgwater in the Civil War. His real armour is on display above the figure.

The villages to the north-west of Swindon take on a different character as the land slopes gently down to the Thames valley. **Highworth** is only a few miles outside Swindon. As the name suggests it stands on a hill and it is claimed that three counties may be seen from here. There are several old buildings round the square, which is the centre of the town. Just behind the shopping centre is a fine Perpendicular church. It dates from the fifteenth century and has many interesting features. Among them is a cannon ball which struck the church during the Civil War. The church was fortified during this period but was stormed by Fairfax.

It is a pleasant drive along the B4019 to **Broad Blunsdon**. Here the church is early English and a lane leads from the church to Castle Hill, an early earthwork fortification. Then cross the dual carriageway of the A419, taking the road to **Blunsdon St Andrew**, past the speedway stadium. The tiny church here is thirteenth century and alongside it are the ruins of Blunsdon Abbey, which burnt down some years ago. The grounds are now a caravan park. Continue along the minor road towards Purton, but at the first crossroads turn north towards Cricklade.

Cricklade and the surrounding area is dominated by the magnificent Tudor tower of St Sampson's Church. St Sampson was a Breton saint who was born in 465. Parts of the church are much older than the tower. There are nave arches dating from the twelfth, thirteenth and fourteenth centuries and there are transepts in the south chapel dating from the fifteenth century. The church has an Elizabethan altar table. Also in the town is the smaller Church of St Mary, at the north end of the High Street. The village holds a words festival and music festival, the latter being held in St Sampson's Church in September.

Cricklade lies just off Ermine Street (now the A419) and was a Roman settlement. King Alfred visited here and Robert Jenner, a London goldsmith, founded a school here in 1651. Near St Mary's Church a group of buildings known as The Priory include the remains of a thirteenth-century hospital. There is a small museum in Calcutt Street, opposite the colourful clock tower, which houses varying local exhibitions which have from time to time included toys and a Victorian kitchen.

The infant River Thames flows under the bridge at the north end of the High Street. Just over the Thames but just before a hump-backed bridge there is a stile on the left and an obvious footpath. This leads toward North Meadow, one of the finest remaining examples of ancient meadowland. It was made a nature reserve in 1973. There are some old marker stones remaining and some rare plants. Please respect the reserve and leave the plants for others to admire. By following the path upstream to a footbridge, it is possible to cross the Thames and return on the other bank.

For people with a taste for ambling through the villages, a pleasant motor tour out from Cricklade can be made. Back onto the A419 turn south for Swindon but take the first left turn to **Castle Eaton**, which has an attractive little thirteenth-century church, and the Red Lion which has gardens beside the Thames. Leave the village to go north to **Marston Meysey**, which straggles along its only street. This is probably the most northerly village in Wiltshire. There are some fine old houses, only glimpsed from the road, and there is an inviting looking pub called The Spotted Cow and Calf which also has a restaurant. Near Marston Meysey there is also a round house and a canal bridge. There is an alternative return to Cricklade.

Leave Cricklade by the B4040 road towards Malmesbury. One mile outside the town turn right towards Ashton Keynes. For lovers of ancient churches there is a small gem in the form of The Old Chancel, All Saints Church, The Leigh. Along the Ashton Keynes road the Thames is crossed at Waterhay Bridge, unmistakable as it carries its name on a board. Do not cross this bridge but turn left. In 400m there is a sign pointing to the right down a track 'footpath to the Church'. 400m down this track is the Old Chancel. The original building is probably thirteenth century but was much reconstructed in 1370 and 1450. There is some detail to interest the dedicated. In 1896 a new church was built in **Leigh**, half a mile away, as in wet weather it was often difficult to reach the church because of floods. The Chancel has been redundant since 1976 and has been in the care of the Redundant Churches Fund since 1978.

Retrace the way back to Waterhay Bridge and turn left at the junction, to cross the bridge and soon reach **Ashton Keynes**. Claimed as the first Thames village its lovely old Cotswold stone cottages glow golden in the sunlight. It is well worth walking round to admire the attractive cottages and gardens. Almost all in one road seem to have their own bridge across the Thames, leading to the front door. The houses in Church Walk, Ashton Mill and Brook House are fine examples. There are four ancient crosses, three in the village, by the White Hart, the Smith's shop and at the start of Church Walk. The fourth cross has been restored and stands in the churchyard as a war memorial. There is some evidence of a twelfth-century origin in the church but it is mainly thirteenth. The farm-house by the church is the only remnant of a vanished monastery.

This area of north-west Wiltshire has some interesting industrial archaeology. West Mill Lane in Cricklade is the site of West Mill Wharf, which was on the North Wiltshire branch of the Wiltshire and Berkshire Canal. It has been mostly filled in. Just to the north, near Latton on the A419, Latton Basin can still be seen. This was the junction of the Wiltshire and Berkshire Canal with the Thames and Severn Canal. One mile north-west, there is a footpath along the old canal route, near **Cerney Wick**, where there is an old round house, similar to the one at Marston Meysey (they were typical of this canal), which was the lock keeper's cottage, and the remains of the lock.

Coming a lot more up to date is the **Cotswold Water Park**, where there is every imaginable recreational facility. Here in the broad upper Thames valley, gravel has been recovered from a vast area, leaving over a hundred lakes. Some of course are small, little more than ponds, and others are huge. The area designated as the Cots-wold Water Park spreads across a vast area crossing the border into Gloucestershire both to the east and west of Ashton Keynes. The landscape is typical lowland broad river valley, though the villages are still characteristic of the Cotswold style. There are many foot-paths (with a programme of guided walks), and nature reserves, both public and private. Additionally there is every type of water-borne sport and many of the clubs offer day membership, or boats, sailboards or water skis may be hired. There are boat trips as well. The area is so vast that the activities are well spaced out and rarely intrude upon each other. Many of the lakes have had some time to mature and it should not be supposed that these are mere gravel pits. They are beautiful lakes with mature trees and shrubs abound-ing, making the nature reserves and picnic areas delightful.

Leave the Ashton Keynes area by going north, appropriately via North End, to a crossroads. Here turn left, in and out of Gloucester-shire, past the turning to Somerford Keynes and follow the minor road to **Oaksey**. This straggling village has some interesting seven-teenth-century cottages, the remains of a Norman motte and bailey castle known as Norwood Castle (this lies to the north of the village near Dean Farm and is on private land), and a small thirteenth- century church with some fragments of medieval paintings. On the south wall a painting of the *Christ of Trades* shows our Lord surrounded by tools, suggesting the moral that salvation lies in labour. There were many more oak trees around the village formerly and the name may have originated there. The village and the manor are the home of Lord Oaksey, the John Oaksey of television commentary, who farms in the area.

Follow the signposts, in a southerly direction, from Oaksey to Eastcourt, on to Hankerton and crossing the B4040 near Charlton continue to **Garsdon**. The roads are narrow but fairly quiet and the gentle meander will be its own reward. The village church here holds the 'Stars and Stripes' tomb. Long before the Stars and Stripes became the flag of America they adorned the tomb of Laurence Washington who was interred here in 1640. The Washington family bought the manor of Garsdon from one Richard Moody, who was given the gift of the manor by Henry VIII. The story goes that Richard Moody helped Henry VIII up after the king had fallen in mud so deep he could not extricate himself. Richard Moody gave the bells to the church. Long ago the memorial was found broken but was restored early in this century by the Bishop of New York and American friends.

It is not far to the attractive stone-built hill town of **Malmesbury**, one of the oldest boroughs in England, which became rich through the weaving trade. There are sixteenth- and seventeenth-century houses, while the Old Bell Hotel and St John's Almshouses include windows from the thirteenth century. The Old Bell stands in the precinct of Malmesbury Abbey, and dating from 1220, is said to be the oldest in England, having been built as a guest house for visitors and pilgrims to the abbey. At the top of the High Street stands a fine and elaborate sixteenth-century market cross.

The most important building in the town is the parish church, originally part of Malmesbury Abbey. Although the abbey ruins are but a fraction of their original size, what remains of the abbey church is most impressive. The doorway of the south porch has some of the finest Norman sculpture in Britain. In the church is the (empty) fifteenth-century tomb of King Athelstan, the first king of all England. Athelstan, who was the grandson of Alfred the Great, made Malmesbury his capital. After the Dissolution of the Monasteries the abbey was used for weaving by a Master Stumpe, a rich clothier, and it is due to him that it was turned into a noble parish church.

Thomas Hobbes, who wrote *Leviathan*, was born in Malmesbury, as was a monk who tried to fly from the church tower with wings tied to his hands and ended up being lame for the rest of his life for his pains. In the churchyard lies Hannah Twynoy, who met her end by a 'Tyger fierce' in 1703. In the town hall is the Athelstan Museum with displays of local history.

Heading east from Malmesbury along the B4042 towards **Wootton Bassett**. Soon after passing under the motorway there is a picnic site on the right, or south, of the road. A right turn at the roundabout leads down into the centre of this bustling little town. There are several shops and hostelries along the main street but down near the junction of the B4041 is the old town hall. This quaint little building is raised high on stone posts. It contains the local museum in the upper room and of course, the space beneath must have been used as a market. Now there is an old pair of stocks there. By retracing the route to the roundabout and taking the B4041 towards Purton and then taking the first right, you will arrive at **Lydiard Park**. This is an imposing eighteenth-century mansion set in over 260 acres of parkland, and was the former home of the St John family. There are many valuable and historic objects in its elegant rooms. There is a visitor centre which houses changing displays on conservation, natural history and the local wildlife. There are sweeping lawns and extensive woods. Children will be delighted with the woods to play in and explore but there are also two special play areas, including an almost life-size western fort.

The village of **Lydiard Tregoze** does not now exist, but it had its origins in Saxon times. The lovely St Mary's church remains however, and has many fine features, including the Golden Cavalier, a life-size figure of Edward St John, who was killed in the Civil War. One of the St John family who married in 1440 became the grandmother of the Tudor dynasty. Her daughter, by the Duke of Somerset, was Margaret Countess of Richmond and mother of Henry VII. Perhaps the outstanding memory of the church is that it is full of colour. There are some fine stained glass windows.

It is not far from Lydiard back into **Swindon**. This busy town, the fastest growing in Europe so it is said, has a lot to offer visitors. There is a splendid shopping precinct, with Regent Street and the Brunel shopping centre as the major parts. Quite near the centre of town is Queen's Park where there is a superb display all year round. In Old Town there is a fine example of a Victorian-style park, where over 12 acres offer the chance of a pleasant evening stroll. There are also excellent displays in both Penhill Park and Faringdon Road Park. This last was the first of the town's parks, originally created by the Great Western Railway Company.

Coate Water near Swindon

Swindon is also well catered for with arts facilities. There is the Wyvern Theatre, a luxury complex of 650 seats, where a tremendous variety of performances take place from pre-West End dramas to ballet and pop concerts. The Arts Centre seats 200 and is the home of many smaller cultural groups, but there is also a series of monthly concerts during winter months. The Link Arts Studio at the Link Centre has a 200-seat theatre and Thamesdown Community Arts at the Jolliffe Studio (at the Wyvern Theatre) have facilities for visual arts and crafts and (at the Town Hall Studios) for dance and media arts.

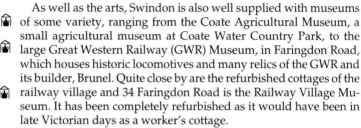

As well as the arts, Swindon is also well supplied with museums of some variety, ranging from the Coate Agricultural Museum, a small agricultural museum at Coate Water Country Park, to the large Great Western Railway (GWR) Museum, in Faringdon Road, which houses historic locomotives and many relics of the GWR and its builder, Brunel. Quite close by are the refurbished cottages of the railway village and 34 Faringdon Road is the Railway Village Museum. It has been completely refurbished as it would have been in late Victorian days as a worker's cottage.

In the Bath Road is the Swindon Museum and Art Gallery. Here there are loan exhibitions from national sources as well as natural history and geological collections. The Art Gallery houses Swindon's art collections and also has local amateur exhibitions. There is also a museum dedicated to the life and work of the naturalist and writer, Richard Jefferies, housed in the actual farmhouse where he was born.

Just south of Swindon on the top of the first step of the Downs is **Wroughton Airfield**, reached via the A361 Swindon to Devizes road. It is a branch of the Science Museum. Here there are major national collections both in store and on display. In two hangers of the old airfield are civil and commercial aircraft, aero-engines, space rockets, hovercraft, marine engines, fire fighting and service vehicles. Another hanger houses a road transport collection which includes buses, steam and motor lorries, cars and carriages, cycles and motor cycles. Opening is limited to special days as it is primarily a storage facility.

In addition to the collections there are other interesting features around the airfield (linked by the perimeter track road which is 6.5km [4 miles] long). In another hanger there is a collection of farm machinery: balers, tractors, ploughs, steam traction engines, carts, wagons and implements. Outside, there is the Butser Ancient Farm Project, a demonstration railway line and throughout the year special open days which have, in the past, staged a kite-fly, the air-Britain-fly-in which had 150 light aircraft attending, a micro-light and flex-wing weekend, a classic car rally and various other car and lorry rallies. The airfield was started in 1940 as an RAF maintenance unit, and lasted until 1978 when it became a Royal Naval Aircraft yard. Though part of the Navy yard remains, the airfield closed and in 1980 the Science Museum took over. Close by this historic airfield is Clouts Wood nature reserve and nature trail.

There are two large sports centres. The Link has ice skating, swimming, squash and lots more. The Oasis has a fun pool with a wave machine and giant waterslides. Both the Link and the Oasis have health suites. In addition there are smaller sports centres round the area, golf courses nearby, riding schools and country parks to get out and about in. The country parks are Coate Water, which offers boating, walks, fishing, mini-golf and picnic area, Lydiard Park, offering walks and picnic area, and the Barbary Castle Country Park on the Ridgeway just south of the town. Barbary Castle is a fine place to blow the cobwebs away when there is a breeze, and the views from the ramparts of the earthwork are fantastic.

Additional Information

Accommodation

£££ = expensive
££ = moderate
£ = inexpensive
EM = evening meal available

Avebury

Mr & Mrs P. Randerson (£, EM)
Winterbourne Monkton, SN4 9NN
☎ 01672 539446

Cricklade

The White Hart Hotel (££, EM)
High Street, SN6 6AA
☎ 01793 750206

Marlborough

Castle & Ball Hotel (£££, EM)
High Street, SN8 1LZ
☎ 01672 515201

Ogborne St George

Parklands Hotel (££, EM)
SN8 1SL
☎ 01672 841555

Laurel Cottage (£)
Southend, SN8 1SG
☎ 01672 841288

Swindon

The School House Hotel & Restaurant (£££, EM)
Hook Street, Hook, SN4 8EF
☎ 01793 851198

Moormead Country Hotel (£££/££ weekends, EM)
Moormead Road, Wroughton, SN4 9BY
☎ 01793 814744

Places to Visit

Avebury

Alexander Keiller Museum (NT)
☎ 01672 539250
Open: April-October daily 10am-6pm (or dusk if earlier), November-March daily 10am-4pm. Closed 24-6 December, 1 January.

Wiltshire Rural Life Exhibition
Great Barn, SN8 1RF
☎ 01672 539555
Open: daily mid-March to mid-November, 10am-5.30pm. Mid November to mid-March weekends 11am-4.30pm.

Avebury Manor (NT)
☎ 016723 539388
Garden open: April-October daily except Monday & Thursday 11am-5.30pm; open Bank Holiday Monday.
Telephone to check opening times of house.

Coate

Agricultural Museum
Coate Water Country Park
Open: Easter-October, Sunday 2-5pm. Other times by appointment.

Cricklade

Cricklade Museum
Calcutt Street
☎ 01793 750756
Open: Wednesday 2-4pm and Saturday 10am-12noon.

Malmesbury

Athelstan Museum
Town Hall, Cross Hayes, SN16 9BZ
Open: April- September Tuesday-Sunday 10.30am-12.30pm, 1-4pm; October-March Wednesday, Friday & Saturday 1-3pm.

Swindon

Great Western Railway Museum
Faringdon Road, SN1 5BJ
☎ 01793 493189
Open: Monday-Saturday 10am-5pm, Sunday 2-5pm.

Lydiard Park
Lydiard Tregoze SN5 9PA
☎ 01793 770401
House open: Monday-Saturday, 10am-1pm and 2-5.30pm, Sunday 2-5.30pm. November-February closes at 4.30pm.

Railway Village Museum
34 Faringdon Road SN1 5BJ
☎ 01793 526161 extension 4527
Open: Monday-Saturday 10am-1pm, 2-5pm, Sunday 2-5pm.

Richard Jefferies Museum
☎ 01793 26161 ext3130
Open: Wednesday, Saturday and Sunday 2-5pm.

Swindon Museum & Art Gallery
Bath Road, SN1 4BA
☎ 01793 493188
Open: Monday-Saturday 10am-5pm, Sunday 2-5pm. Admission free.

Wroughton

Science Museum
☎ 01793 813569
Open: May-September on selected weekends. Transport, air museum, agricultural machinery.

Tourist Information Centres

Avebury
☎ 016723 452

Malmesbury
Town Hall, SN16 9BZ
☎ 01666 823748

Marlborough
☎ 01672 53989

Swindon
☎ 01793 30328

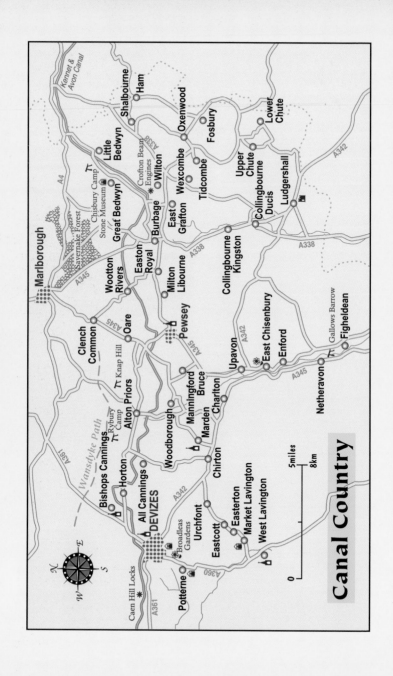

Canal Country

Canal Country

9

Between the Wansdyke Path to the north and the wild area of Salisbury Plain to the south, is the tranquil and gentle Vale of Pewsey.

The Kennet and Avon Canal climbs up the hill at Devizes then wends its way through some splendid countryside just a mile or so south of the Downs with some splendid views to the north of the escarpment. Winding onwards and upwards to Crofton, where the great beam engine still occasionally pumps water, the canal leaves Wiltshire near Froxfield.

Upavon guards the route dividing Salisbury Plain where the A345 runs alongside the River Avon. **Pewsey** is the central point of this area, a pleasant little town which was once owned by King Alfred. The church stands on sarsen stones laid by the Saxons. It has a fifteenth-century tower and the altar rail is made from timbers from the *San Josef*, a three-deck ship captured by Nelson in 1797. A statue of King Alfred stands at the crossroads and there are some nice old houses. Pewsey is famous for its carnival, held in September, which is claimed as the 'mother of West Country carnivals'.

Half a mile north of the town is Pewsey Wharf where the old wharf, canal house and adjoining warehouse are often complemented by an attractive gathering of boats. To the west, by about a mile along the canal, is **Wilcot**. This attractive village straddles the canal and spreads round the village green to the pub while the group of old houses round the church are almost a separate hamlet. Wilcot and the now vanished vineyards are mentioned in the Domesday Book. This ancient record claims 'a new church, a very good house, a good vineyard'.

Those walking the towpath to Wilcot will pass the attractive Stowell Park where a miniature suspension bridge was built in the nineteenth century to carry a private footpath over the canal.

Another mile west along the canal is Ladies' Bridge. This is a particularly decorative stone bridge built by Rennie in 1808. It is unique in that such elaborate designs were usually confined to major works. On the way a handsome wooden swing bridge is passed which moves easily on its bearings.

Continue along the A345 in a northerly direction to arrive at the village of **Oare** and Oare House, where the gardens only are open to the public on Sundays in April and July. There are fine trees, extensive lawns and a kitchen garden. About a mile to the west is the hamlet of **Draycot FitzPayne** where the manor house also opens its gardens once or twice a year under the National Gardens Scheme.

On the way up Oare Hill the magnificently sited Rainscombe House can be seen to the right from the road. At the top of this long hill there is a parking area and to the east of the road is Martinsell Hill with an ancient Iron Age hillfort. There are excellent views from the southern edge.

By proceeding further north to Clench Common a right turn on minor roads leads back down to **Wootton Rivers** and the canal again. There is an attractive setting of locks near the road bridge at the southern end of the village. However, the interesting feature of this attractive village is Jack Spratt's clock. This local craftsman made the clock from scrap and odds and ends found locally. In the place of numerals the letters spell out 'Glory be to God'.

Just a little farther along the canal the A346 crosses near Burbage Wharf and just over half a mile beyond that is the Bruce Tunnel. The tunnel portals are brick and carry a memorial plaque to Thomas

previous page: Pewsey Wharf

Bruce, Earl of Aylesbury and to Charles, Lord Bruce, his son. The tunnel is 460m (1,509ft) long and boats were pulled through by hand using chains fixed to the walls.

Burbage is just to the south, the main part of the old village being just off the new main road. Close by is Wolfhall, a private dwelling standing on the site of the residence of the Seymours of Savernake, where Henry VIII came to court Jane Seymour.

The B3087 leads back towards Pewsey passing a turning to **Easton Royal**, a pretty hamlet lying quietly to the south of the road. Next is **Milton Lilbourne** also to the south of the B3087, peacefully straggling down its main street. With old cottages on high pavements all round and a fine old church, it is a very pleasant backwater. A good walk can be made southwards up to Milton Hill, joining a farm road near Milton Hill Farm before turning north again and passing close to Giant's Grave long barrow before descending to the valley again. The Giant's Grave is a Neolithic long barrow, which was excavated by John Thurnam. Built of chalk, it represented a burial of three or four people. On the return, on reaching the infant River Avon, turn right upstream on the south bank for almost a mile to re-enter the village.

Back at Burbage, take the A338 in an easterly direction. Soon there are signposts for Wilton Windmill and Crofton Pumping Station.

Crofton Pumping Station on the Kennet and Avon Canal shows a fine example of engineering craftsmanship. It is claimed to have the oldest working beam engines 'in steam' in the world. One was built in 1812 by Boulton and Watt and one in 1845 by Harveys of Hayle. They were installed to pump water to the top section of the canal and of course they have been restored. Pumping is now done by electric motor but these great engines are in steam on some summer weekends. The site is also open on Sundays from April to October. Other attractions are working models and canal trips on the narrow boat *Jubilee*, which actually goes through the tunnel. Because of the limited opening a preliminary enquiry is best.

By returning through East Grafton, or perhaps even better, by taking the footpath beside Wilton water, the village of **Wilton** can be reached. A charming village where streams run through the gardens, eventually feeding the duck pond, and with lots of thatched cottages. On a hill to the east is Wilton Windmill. The mill was built in 1821. It fell into disuse near the end of the century and was restored in 1976. It is now in full working order and is claimed to be Wiltshire's only working windmill, producing stoneground wholemeal flour. It is open on Sundays and Bank Holidays.

Bridge over the Kennet and Avon Canal

Continue along the minor road and turn north to **Great Bedwyn**. Bedwyn is also in the Domesday Book , when it had 'land for eighty ploughs, less one'. The village was once larger than it is now and must have prospered for some time. Both the canal and the railway brought trade, and the railway station is still open.

Close to the wharf, in Brook Street, is a basket maker where all kinds of basketry may be bought, or made to order.

Cross the canal and the railway from the wharf and turn down Church Street. There is a Stone Museum along here where they kindly allow access to view the exhibits. In normal business hours, stonemasons may be seen at work. It is only a few steps from here along to the church which is well worth visiting, as it contains the tomb of Sir John Seymour, father of Jane Seymour, wife of Henry VIII.

Little Bedwyn lies a mile from Great Bedwyn and between the two, on a hill, is Chisbury Camp, an Iron Age hillfort. Within the ramparts are the remains of a chapel, now used as a farm building. The east window still has its beautiful fourteenth-century tracery.

A battle was fought here 1,300 years ago and this area had a Saxon mint and a Roman camp. The great stone spire of the church is a

The pub at Ham

landmark in the surrounding countryside, it was built by the Norman masons who built the church at Great Bedwyn.

To the south-east and across the A338 is **Shalbourne**, a pleasant village sitting round the village green, which it shares with the local pub. At the far end there is a footpath to the church and access is also by road a little way on. It was probably built late in the twelfth century with the tower being fifteenth century.

Following minor roads leads to the tiny hamlet of **Ham**, with some attractive thatched cottages, a pub near the small green and a tiny church which is rather special because of its simplicity.

From Ham follow the byways south-west by way of Ham Hill, Fosbury and Oxenwood to **Tidcombe**, where a charming (private) Queen Anne house stands near the flint and rubble Norman church. Tidcombe lies just off the Roman road that ran up to Marlborough before making the great sweep round that is known as Chute Causeway. Tidcombe sits below the Downs and there are prehistoric remains all round. Towbarrow is on Wexcombe Down, a mile west, there is a long barrow half a mile south, another a mile north-east and all around there are tumuli and earthworks, with tracks and paths in plenty from which to view them.

By following Chute Causeway south then turning right, **Upper**

Chute and **Lower Chute** may be found hiding away in the remains of Chute Forest, which was named in the Domesday Book. It must then have been indistinguishable from Collingbourne Forest which is just a little way to the west.

More minor roads south then west soon arrive at the A342 and **Ludgershall**. This is a long straggling village but is worth a look round. Protected by railings made by the village blacksmith long ago is the stump of an ancient cross. Ludgershall was a Saxon stronghold before the Normans took over and built a castle on the same site. The ruins of that castle can be viewed and a pleasant walk can be made beyond the castle, to the north, in Collingbourne Forest. The castle was 'royal', a governor being appointed by the king. It was in ruins by the sixteenth century and it is said that Queen Maud sought sanctuary there from King Stephen. The church is Norman and has a fine canopied tomb of Sir Richard Brydges and his wife.

Leaving Ludgershall by the A338 Marlborough Road, the road soon arrives at **Collingbourne Ducis**. The church is described as thirteenth century, but that was its first rebuilding; the Domesday Book describes the church as being in ruins. It contains tombs of the Seymour family and there was renovation in Victorian times.

Just over a mile north is **Collingbourne Kingston**. Both villages derive part of their names from the River Bourne which runs down their valley. Return via Burbage to Pewsey and take a left turn onto the A345 but in just under 2 miles, turn right on a minor road to **Manningford Bruce**. For the Norman church and Manningford Bruce House, which opens its gardens occasionally, take the next right after the village sign from the main road. Inside the church is a memorial to Mary Nicholas, who helped her sister Jane Lane to assist King Charles II to safety after the battle at Worcester in 1651. Jane rode pillion dressed as a groom to guide the king along roads which swarmed with Parliamentarian troops eager to find him.

From Pewsey the A345 leads in a southerly direction again to **Upavon**, a quiet village on the banks of the River Avon. This was the birthplace of Henry Hunt, later known as 'Orator Hunt' and Member of Parliament for Preston in 1830.

On the Downs to the south-east lies Upavon airfield, where the Central Flying School of the Royal Flying Corps was opened in 1912. Above the village, to the south-west, is **Casterly Camp**, the largest prehistoric fortress in Wiltshire. It is little over a mile from the road and a bridleway leads up to it. There are extensive views south over Salisbury Plain or north over Pewsey Vale.

Leave Upavon by the A342 Andover Road and after half a mile go straight ahead on a minor road to reach **East Chisenbury**, where Chisenbury Priory opens its gardens on Wednesdays. The fine medieval priory is not open but the 5 acres of gardens with herbaceous borders, mature trees, lawns and shrubs, a water section and a vineyard can be seen and cream teas may also be enjoyed. To the south of the house is the Gladiators' Walk, a deep earthwork with trees on its banks.

Follow the minor road south where, in the fertile valley, the villages gather, protected by the great rise of the plain on either hand. The parish boundaries here run up the slopes. That way each had some of the high grazing but each also had some of the rich land along the river banks. The hamlets of **Enford**, **Fittleton**, **Netheravon** and **Figheldean** shelter down here on this quiet byway. All have ancient churches but all have older histories. Gallows Barrow stands beside the road between Netheravon and Figheldean, while across the river is the site of a Roman villa.

Regaining the main road go north, back towards the Vale of Pewsey. It is easy to miss the turning to **Charlton**, birthplace of Stephen Duck, a thresher who became a 'Peasant Poet' in the eighteenth century. He received the patronage of Queen Charlotte but met with an untimely end. Two more miles along the pleasant A342 is **Chirton**, a pleasing village of Georgian buildings, a thatched cottage and well trimmed grass verges. Chirton church sits on a mound at the end of the village; from the well kept churchyard there is an excellent view northwards. Nearby is **Conock**, unusual in that it has two manor houses. The brick Old Manor and the Bath stone Conock Manor were both built in the eighteenth century. Very occasionally the gardens of the latter are open to the public.

North-east by a mile is **Marden**, where the Norman church has some later and interesting features: a pinnacled tower, decorated buttresses with panels ending in crocketed pinnacles, a splendidly carved Norman doorway and, inside, the roof of the nave is carried on crowned and mitred heads.

Just over the river is a large earthwork; the whole site is an oval of 35 acres. It is the largest henge monument in Britain and has the unique feature of two entrances at right angles to each other, on the north and east sides. Once a great mound, Hatfield Barrow, stood inside the earthwork. Claimed to be 62m (200ft) in diameter and nearly 16m (50ft) high, it has since been ploughed away. The henge itself was excavated in 1969 near the northern entrance, but no spectacular finds were made.

The white horse at Alton Barnes

Follow the minor road northwards, crossing the railway near Woodborough and the canal again at **Honeystreet**. Here there was a wharf and a canal community. The Canal Inn is still there and still open for business. There is an industrial site and the works chimney still stands.

From the canal bridge there is a fine view of the Alton Barnes white horse and that mysterious line of hills so full of ancient sites, but before the hills, turn down to the Saxon church at **Alton Barnes**. There is a footpath over the fields to another church about a quarter of a mile away at **Alton Priors**. The earliest mention of Alton Priors was in 835. When King Egbert beat the Mercians at Wroughton he gave land in the village to the cathedral of Winchester.

In 1830 a mob, incensed by the introduction of agricultural machinery, arrived at the rectory and manor adjacent to St Mary's at Alton Barnes. They wounded a friend of the rector and militia were dispatched from Marlborough and Devizes to quell the riot.

A left turn at the next junction leads along a very pleasant minor road back towards Devizes. Here, between the A342 and the hills, there are several villages, all worthy of a visit to enjoy the sleepy peace of the area. All have histories and stories. Some, like **All Cannings**, give their name to a stretch of downland. On All

Cannings Down there was a British settlement dated 600BC. A Captain Cunningham made notable discoveries in 1920. Anthony Methuen was rector of the village church for 60 years and his friend, the poet Coleridge, stayed with him there for an extended visit.

Bishops Cannings church spans the centuries, with a twelfth-century beginning and a fifteenth-century spire. The entrance porch has fourteenth-century mouldings.

There are several good tracks going up the hillside to the north to reach the **Wansdyke Path** which runs along the ridge. This magnificent ancient defensive earthwork is still a spectacular sight. Constructed about AD577 by the west Saxons, it was once about 50 miles in length. A good section in each direction can be seen from the A361 at Shepards Shore about 3 miles outside Devizes. However, a walk is the best way to see it, taking in Tan Hill as well. A useful series of walk guide leaflets, including a section of the canal, Wansdyke and Tan Hill are available from the Devizes Information Office.

According to John Aubrey, Tan Hill is a corruption of St Anne's Hill. For as long as anyone can remember a great sheep fair was held on Tan Hill. Traders gathered here from far and near to trade and barter sheep and oxen. The police often had to restrain a few

The Cramer, Devizes

revellers. The downfall of the fair came one wet summer. For a year or so the newly invented motors had had difficulty in getting up the slippery chalk, and one very wet summer many were bogged down, after which the fairs ceased.

There is a dew pond up here, a remnant of a dying art. High up on the sheep pastures the chalk drys quickly and there are no springs to water the stock. Dew ponds were the answer. To create a dew pond a round shallow pit was dug, lined quite thickly with straw, then covered with clay, which had to be hauled in. The clay had to be 'puddled' into a sticky mass then smoothed to form a water-tight lining. Condensation plays a part in keeping the dew pond full; the straw retains heat and the cool of the night allows dew to condense. Rain also helps of course, but an undamaged dew pond never drys out, even in very dry spells of weather.

Rybury Camp is just on the edge of the hill. It has been suggested that the Iron Age fort overlays a Neolithic camp. It was just south of here that the All Cannings finds were made.

Crossing and recrossing the canal and passing through Horton on the way, the minor road reaches the A361; turn left here for Devizes.

Devizes, it has been said, is the only market town in Wiltshire without an ancient history. The town did not exist before the Norman conquest. Bishop Osmund built Devizes Castle in 1080. It was built of wood and it burnt down. Bishop Roger rebuilt it in stone in 1138. After a long and often turbulent history it was eventually dismantled by parliament after it was besieged and surrendered to Cromwell in 1645. The present castle was built in the nineteenth century and is not open to the public.

There are many treasures in Devizes, ranging from the gardens, the many fine and historical buildings, the museum and canal centre, to the splendid churches.

St John's Church was built in 1150 by Bishop Roger as the church for the castle and the original typically Norman plan was changed in the fifteenth century when the nave was rebuilt. St John's also has many interesting memorials but the churchyard must be inspected. Apart from the many interesting tombs there are the old houses round about including the seventeenth-century sexton's house.

St Mary's in New Park Street was also built by Bishop Roger in 1150. St James', Southbroom, built in the fifteenth century, still bears the scars of Cromwell's cannon ball, inflicted during the Civil War. There are also other churches and chapels in the town.

Long Street, beyond St John's, has a long line of Georgian houses and also has the Devizes Museum. The latter is a splendid museum considering the size of the town. Visitors from far afield are drawn here by the outstanding prehistoric collections from the county. Weapons, jewellery, tools, metalwork and pottery record and illustrate history and progress in Wiltshire from the earliest times until the Romans. There are exhibits from all the major archaeological digs in the county: Avebury, Woodhenge, West Kennet long barrow and many others. There are exhibits from the Bronze Age which are of particular importance, including rich grave finds.

Exhibits do not stop at the ancient, others continue up to Saxon times and the recent history gallery describes the the town from its beginnings to the present day. A natural history gallery explains how man has influenced the habitats of the chalk down and farmlands. The art gallery has regularly changing exhibitions from the town's own collection or with works by local artists.

On the wharf the work of the Kennet and Avon Canal Trust may be seen. The canal was the work of engineer John Rennie. It linked London and Bristol and was once a hive of industry. The rebuilt wharf houses not only the Canal Museum, but also the local information office and the Wharf Theatre.

A good walk can be taken along the canal westwards to inspect the Caen Hill flight of locks, the most famous in Britain and a magnificent feat of engineering. Here sixteen closely built locks climb a steep hill towards the town centre. After extensive restoration work on the lock gates the canal has been restored to full navigation. Alongside each lock is a large pond, more like a reservoir, and the area is a wonderful habitat for wildlife. A leaflet on the locks makes the walk more interesting. It explains all the points of note along the whole of the Devizes flight of twenty-nine locks.

At the Lower Wharf, Northgate Street, is the working canal forge. Though the fire is not always in use there is an exhibition of blacksmith's tools and a display of hand-forged iron work.

Of the many fine buildings listed in the town's own leaflet which is obtainable at the information office, several can be seen from the market place. The town hall, the corn exchange and the Bear Hotel, which is an old coaching inn dating back to 1590, can all be seen from the foot of the market cross. One panel of the market cross tells the story of Ruth Pierce. When she was accused of cheating on a deal on her market stall she said 'May I drop down dead if I am lying'. She promptly fell dead on the spot.

Devizes is also supposedly the origin of the 'Moonrakers' story. Smugglers were almost caught by the excise men, they dropped the brandy cask in the Crammer Pond (the pool by St James' Church)

Devizes wharf

and were raking the water when the excise men found them. When asked what they were doing, they said they were trying to rake the cheese off the water. The 'cheese' was the reflection of the moon.

Devizes has a theatre at which there are a variety of entertainments. It is a in well-converted canal warehouse on the wharf. Hillforth Park has some beautifully cultivated lawns and flower beds. There are also public tennis courts available.

A fine walk from the town centre is along Quaker's Walk and up Roundway Down. Leave the town by way of Park Bridge, over the canal and through a splendid pair of ornamental wrought iron gates. A fine copse of beech trees crowns Roundway Hill. Beyond, on the flatter ground, the Battle of Roundway Down was fought in 1643. On the south-western escarpment is Roundway Hill covert which holds a nature trail and just beyond that is Oliver's Castle, an Iron Age hillfort which commands extensive views. For the less active this area can be reached by car. The last section towards Oliver's Castle is an unsurfaced track but there is room to park and turn round.

Broadleas Gardens 1½ miles away on the A360 are open to the public. Broadleas is the home of Lady Anne Cowdray and the gardens have been developed over the last 30 years to include some rare and unusual plants. There is a woodland walk, winter garden, rose garden, herbaceous border, arboretum and azalea terrace.

Not far south-east of Devizes is the village of **Urchfont**. The duckpond and ducks, with a fine house and trees beyond, make a pretty picture. Locals can still remember times when villagers took it in turns to stay up, with a shotgun, guarding the ducks against marauding foxes. William Pitt once owned the William and Mary manor house which is now a college. The name of the village is said to derive from the spring (fount) of Urch, which never dried out even in very hot summers. Wiltshire Folk Life Society's *Urchfont, a Brief History* gives a good list of the various occupations in the village a century ago. It was almost self-sufficient, having all the required trades: tailor, shoemaker, builder, wheelwright, carriers, thatchers, a rat catcher, forge, mills and seven inns or public houses.

From Urchfont it is possible to drive up via Redborn Hill, south-east from the village, onto the edge of Salisbury Plain. Along the escarpment the military authority has allowed access and an unsurfaced road has been laid, so it is possible to drive from the A342 to the A360 at St Joan a Gores cross. The route allows extensive views across the plain which is used as a military training area. This is claimed as part of the route of the traditional Ridgeway and is incorporated in the extension of the Ridgeway Path from Overton Hill, near Avebury, down to Lyme Regis, the section called the Wessex Ridgeway. The Ramblers' Association did a lot of work towards the opening of this route, but they did not envisage it as a vehicular right of way, only a bridleway.

An alternative route is by way of the B3098, a very pretty road which twists and turns along the bottom of the hill by way of Eastcott, Easterton and the long, straggling village of **Market Lavington**, a bustling village with an air of being lived in, not just a dormitory for town workers; it still has shops and services. It was once, until the nineteenth century, a flourishing market for the sale of sheep and corn. Tom Smiths have lived for over two hundred years in a cottage by the old smithy. For that time the name, and the secret of dew pond making, have been passed down from father to son. There is a Norman church, built in 1349, and village museum in the old schoolmaster's house.

As Market Lavington lies along the B3098, so **West** (formerly Bishops) **Lavington** lies along the A360. Here there are some interesting old buildings near the church, off the main road. Close beside the church is the splendid old manor house adorned by an old wistaria. The church dates from the end of the twelfth century with work from all the great building centuries since then. The Beckett chapel is named for a family who lived in the village. The south chapel was built by the Dauntseys (who founded the school), who were living in the village by 1430. In 1543 the school was founded, and the almshouses to the north-east of the church. They were rebuilt in brick in 1831 and have recently been restored.

South of the church, where White Street comes up from the main road, a track goes south with views across the valley, over the pools below from The Warren to Ram's Cliff. Turn right where the tracks cross; to return to the village, take the next right turn, or to make a longer walk turn right down a field side half a mile on by a copse.

A mile south of the village, on the main road, is the Robber's Stone. Near this spot in 1839 a yeoman farmer, Mr Dean of Imber, was returning home from market in Devizes. He was set upon by four villains. After a spirited chase one of the villains fell dead. The other three were eventually captured, tried and sentenced to 15 years transportation.

Returning to Devizes along the A360 is the village of **Potterne**. St Mary's Church is early English and among its treasures is a font believed to be Saxon. Another treasure in the village is the half-timbered early Tudor Porch House. The house (which can be visited by written appointment) had a chequered career, but it was being used as an inn in 1870 when George Richmond, the portrait painter, bought it and set about restoring it. It is still a private house with old oak furniture in every room, peepholes from the bedrooms down into the great hall and leather thongs to lift the latches on the doors.

In the old coach house of Potterne Manor House, the fire brigade headquarters, the Wiltshire Fire Defence and Brigades Museum offers an insight into this most dangerous of occupations.

Additional Information

Accommodation

£££ = expensive
££ = moderate
£ = inexpensive
EM = evening meal available

All Cannings (near Devizes)

Jean Turner (£, EM)
Corners Cottage, The Street,
SN10 3PA
☎ 01380 860626

Devizes

The Black Swan Hotel (££, EM)
Market Palce, SN10 1JQ
☎ 01380 723259

Rathin Guest House (££, EM)
Wick Lane, SN10 5DP
☎ 01380 721999

Glenholme Guest House (£, EM)
77 Nursteed Road, SN10 3AJ
☎ 01380 723187

Enford
Enford House (£, EM)
Enford, near Pewsey, SN9 6DJ
☎ 01980 670414

Great Bedwyn
The Cross Keys (£, EM)
SN8 3NU
☎ 01672 870678

Pewsey
The Royal Oak (£, EM)
35 North Street, SN9 5ES
☎ 01672 63426

Mrs M. Landless (£)
Follets, Easton Royal, SN9 5LZ
☎ 01672 810619
Eat at the Royal Oak, Wootton Rivers.

Wootton Rivers
The Royal Oak (£, EM)
SN8 4NQ
☎ 01672 810322

Places to Visit

Burbage
Crofton Pumping Station
Alongside Kennet and Avon Canal,
6 miles south-east of Marlborough,
off the A346.
Open: variable, enquire locally. In
steam some days.

Devizes
Broadleas Gardens
Just south of Devizes
☎ 01380 722035
Open: April-October, Sunday,
Wednesday and Thursday, 2-6pm.

Devizes Museum
41 Long Street, SN10 1NS
☎ 01380 727369
Open: Monday-Saturday 10am-
5pm. Closed Bank Holidays.

Kennet & Avon Canal Museum
Canal Centre, Couch Lane, SN10 1EB
☎ 01380 721279/729489
Open: Easter-Xmas daily 10am-5pm.

*Wiltshire Fire Defence & Brigades
 Museum*
Potterne, SN10 5PP
☎ 01380 723601
Open: first Wednesday of the
month or by appointment.
Admission free.

East Grafton
Wilton Windmill
☎ 01672 870268
Open: Easter-September Sunday
and Bank Holidays 2-5pm.

Great Bedwyn
Bedwyn Stone Museum
Back Lane
Open: all year.

Market Lavington
Museum
Church Street
☎ 01380 818736
Open: May-September Wednesday,
Saturday, Sunday & Bank Holidays
2.30-4.30pm or by appointment.

Oare
Oare House
Gardens open: April and July
Sunday 2-6pm.
☎ 01491 874072

Tourist Information Centres

Chippenham
☎ 01249 657733

Devizes
☎ 01380 729408

The Avon Valley

10

Just down the road from Devizes is the bustling little market town of **Melksham**. It is geographically central to this area, so it is a convenient place to use for outings. It is only 10 miles south of junction seventeen on the M4 so access is easy. There is plenty to see in the surrounding area, including very fine manor houses and gardens, lovely old towns and museums, all in splendid countryside.

Melksham's history goes back to before the Domesday Book. At one time it was partly owned by Britric Aluric, a Norman knight. William the Conqueror granted him the villages of Melksham and Paulshot. His name is remembered in Aloeric School. Originally a small village surrounded by forest, which is remembered in the name Forest Road, it was a hunting area but by the seventeenth century most of the forest had been cleared.

above: Lacock Abbey

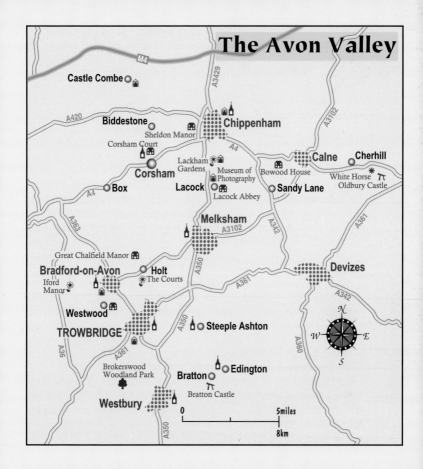

The Avon Valley

In the more recent past Melksham had its own canal. It was part of the Wiltshire and Berkshire Canal which ran from the Kennet and Avon (the junction was at Semington just south of Melksham) to Latton Basin (see Chapter 8), where there was a junction with the Thames and Severn Canal. The Wiltshire and Berkshire Canal was opened in 1819 and was finally abandoned in 1914 after years of disuse. Its course can be traced on maps and in the towns there are signs. Just down Spa Road there is a hump in the road where the canal crossed. Just beyond is Rope Walk, commemorating the rope works of C. W. Maggs and Company who used the canal.

Melksham had a brief spell as a spa town. Saline and chalybeate springs were found and an attempt was made to develop the facility. An elegant pump room was built and lodging houses for the visitors. These elegant houses can still be seen. By 1822 the venture had failed and visitors went to the better known and more fashionable spa at nearby Bath. It could have succeeded as Melksham was on the old stage coach road from London to Bath and was a major stopping place. Some of the old coaching inns remain still, of which the King's Arms is a good example, along with The George, The Bear and The New Crown.

Melksham was a wool town and there are still buildings which survive from this period. The Roundhouse in Church Street dates from the seventeenth century and is now a craft centre and the local information office. At the end of Church Street is the attractive Canon Square which leads off into Church Walk, where some of the town's oldest remaining houses can be seen. They make a picturesque grouping of sixteenth, seventeenth and eighteenth-century houses and cottages.

The parish church of St Michael is fifteenth century. There are gargoyles on the tower (which was moved in 1840) and two grotesque beasts. There are some notable memorials in the church, one to John Buckley and a son, who followed his friend William Penn to Pennsylvania. Another memorial is to a Melksham family — father, mother and six children — who perished in the *Titanic* disaster in 1912. The church has some good glass and carvings.

To the north of the town lie some of Wiltshire's treasures. Nearest to Melksham is the National Trust village of **Lacock**. This fascinating village, mercifully quiet now it is bypassed, is a square of streets, mostly narrow, with only the main street wider, which gives a hint of the days when fairs were held. Lacock was prosperous from the centuries of the wool trade, and a stroll round the streets is a must. The Sign of the Angel is an old inn in a street of attractive mellow cottages. The George is one of the oldest continuously licensed inns in England. It is a living village in which the local residents take pride, yet it is quietly informal.

The church of St Cyriac has many treasures and is well known for the stained glass and for its heraldic work. One of the memorials is a brass dating from the fifteenth century. It is to Robert Baynard and his wife; their fifteen children are depicted kneeling.

Lacock Abbey was founded in 1232, as an abbey for Augustinian nuns, by Ela, Countess of Salisbury. She was only seven when her father died and she became a ward of Richard the Lionheart. He married her to his stepbrother William Longsword. They had several children but he was often away at the wars. After a long absence, his death was assumed but Ela refused to believe it and waited. He returned but died soon afterwards. The grieving Ela waited for her sons to come of age before founding Lacock Abbey. She lived for 35 years after her husband died.

The chapter house and cloisters are preserved from Ela's time, though in later centuries there have been changes, notably under the ownership of Sir William Sharington after the Dissolution. He built a mansion round the nunnery. He also pulled down the convent church and built stables. In the eighteenth century the abbey was given a Gothick appearance so it has become a fascinating blend of architectural evolution, and one of England's most beautiful houses.

William Fox Talbot carried out some of the earliest experiments in photography at Lacock Abbey. He made his first camera in 1835 and the first photograph was taken in Lacock Abbey in the same year. Near the abbey gates there is the Museum of Photography in a sixteenth-century barn. On display are Fox Talbot's first cameras and calotypes, darkroom equipment and letters with the international awards that he won.

Within walking distance, by field path in the direction of Chippenham or by the A350, is **Lackham Gardens and Agricultural Museum**. Here the museum displays old farm machinery and tools. The gardens are packed with interest and there is a picnic site, children's play area and riverside walks.

It is possible to drive by quiet lanes from Lacock up over Bowden Hill, a good viewpoint, to **Sandy Lane**. Just where the A342 is joined, the George Inn sits splendidly at the head of this special little village of pretty houses. Most are thatched and at the opposite end to the George is one of the very few thatched churches remaining in Britain. Just north of Sandy Lane are the famous rhododendron walks of Bowood. The entrance to Bowood itself is at Derry Hill a little further on.

Well hidden in the remnants of Chippenham Forest, one of Britain's medieval forests, is the lovely **Bowood House**, seat of the Earls of Shelburne. This magnificent house is the delightfully proportioned result of many changes in the years since the house was bought in 1754. The displays within the house include a sculpture gallery, an orangery which is now a picture gallery, the library and the laboratory in which Dr Joseph Priestley discovered oxygen gas in 1774. One wing contains a series of exhibition rooms with costumes, jewellery, watercolours and miniatures and a collection of Indiana made by the present earl's great grandfather when he was viceroy in India between 1888 and 1894. There is a restaurant and shop and a most spectacular children's adventure playground.

The park, starting with the rose terraces in front of the house, extends to nearly 100 acres and the visitor is free to roam. Landscaped by Capability Brown, the park contains 160 species of trees and shrubs all of which are labelled, enhancing the interest. There is a lake and a series of cascades, caves and grottos, all in a most beautiful and tranquil setting. There is a garden centre and 12 acres of 'pick your own' fruit and vegetables.

Looking in a direction just south of east from Bowood, one may catch a glimpse of a monument high on Cherhill Down, just as the Marlborough Downs start to rise from the valleys of the Avon. Here, alongside one of the famous white horses of Wiltshire, is the **Lansdown Monument**, a tall obelisk about which there are various stories, one that it marks the highest land between London and Bristol, another that it was erected by a local vicar as a memorial to the prominent family. It was built in 1845 on instructions from the Third Marquis of Lansdown in memory of his ancestor, Sir William Petty. It is now owned by the National Trust and it has been restored. The adjacent White Horse was cut in 1790 by Dr Christopher Alsop of Calne.

From the lay-by on the A4 there are two paths by which closer inspection can be made, and the glorious views enjoyed from the ramparts of Oldbury Castle, an ancient hillfort. **Cherhill** used to be an important staging post. The Black Horse Inn is the only survivor of the coaching inns of the village. There is a fifteenth-century church with a fourteenth-century tower, a haven of peace, hiding round the back lane off the main road. In the eighteenth century there was a notorious collection of thieves and footpads known as the Cherhill Gang. A gibbet was set up on the Beckhampton Road to warn them. They used to strip naked before attacking, in order to be less easily recognizable.

Calne lies next westward along the A4 and was for many years the home of the Harris Bacon factory, which dominated the town centre. Sadly for the prosperity of the town the factory is no more. There is a small memorial to the heyday of the bacon in the form of a bronze pig close to the small shopping precinct. The river flowing through the town is the Marden. Doctor's Pond is a wider part and takes its name from Dr Joseph Priestly who took water samples from there during his experiments at Bowood House. The

Lansdown Arms hotel dominates The Strand, which is the wide area of the A4. This old coaching inn has a pleasing façade and some seventeenth-century windows.

Just a few miles more along the A4 and the ancient market town of **Chippenham** is reached. It was a market town in Saxon times, being the hamlet of *Cyppa*. Alfred the Great had a hunting lodge here, used when hunting in the royal forests of Chippenham or Melksham. Today there is still a thriving market. Buyers come from far and wide on Fridays when one of the biggest cattle markets in the country is held.

There is mention of the town in the Domesday Book, but it actually dates back to AD600 when Cyppa the Saxon started the town. When King Alfred was only 4 years old, in AD853, his sister was married from the royal villa. In AD878 the Danes, under Guthrum, spent the winter in the town and King Alfred went to Athelney. Next spring he returned and defeated the Danes at the battle of Ethandune.

Chippenham was an important town for many years. In 1042

Cherhill Down and the white horse

during the reign of King Edward the Confessor, a document refers to the church owning 100 acres of land.

In St Mary street there are a number of interesting sixteenth- and eighteenth-century houses. Round the Market Place some of the present business premises were once coaching inns and numbers 44-49 used to be The White Hart where General Cromwell stayed in 1649 when on his way to Ireland.

The Yelde Hall is a beautifully restored building, half timbered, which was built about five hundred years ago. The town was the administrative centre for the Chippenham Hundred and the hall was used by the Bailiff and the Burgesses until 1841. After some years as a store, then a fire station, it became a museum in 1963. Various displays of local interest and local records and artifacts make it very interesting. A small room just off the main room was the local lock-up.

St Andrew's Church is the oldest of the four churches, dating back to Saxon times, though little is left of that date. The south aisle and the two chapels are fifteenth century. The chancel has a very fine stained glass window. Lord Hungerford, who held the manor of Chippenham, had the tower rebuilt and though it was rebuilt again in the seventeenth century, it still contains the Hungerford coat of arms on the exterior of the western wall.

St Paul's, in the Malmesbury Road, was completed in 1855 by Sir Giles Gilbert Scott. It is a good example of the Gothic Revival style. St Peter's, on the western side, is a modern church with engraved glass and unusual metalwork among the interesting features of this hexagonal building. St Nicholas' Church on Hardenhuish Hill was built in 1779 to replace a medieval church.

There is a riverside walk near the town bridge and there are facilities for tennis, bowls, swimming, golf and fishing. There is a 'par three' golf course in Monkton Park near the sports complex.

Chippenham has a unique feature in Maud Heath's Causeway. In 1474 Maud Heath, a widow, left land and property to the trustees of Chippenham, for the construction and maintenance of a footpath so that country folk could walk to market dry shod. Maud Heath used to walk daily into Chippenham to sell eggs. In those days the river was wider and the paths muddy and rutted. The causeway can be followed today from Wick Hill through Tytherton and Kellaways then Langley Burrell and onto the Swindon Road and so to the outskirts of the town.

Maud Heath's Monument stands at the top of Wick Hill. She is depicted sitting, with an egg basket, gazing out over the Avon

Valley. A memorial stone is adjacent to Kellaways bridge where the path crosses the River Avon.

On the Bristol side of Chippenham, just off the A420, is **Sheldon Manor**. Chippenham was a royal manor, possibly since Alfred's days. In 1174 it was divided into three, Lowden, Rowden and Sheldon, and with Sheldon went the lordship of the Chippenham Hundred. The manor had various owners, three knights in turn, until it came back to the king in 1231. He granted it to Sir Walter Godarville, a Norman knight who had come to England with Falkes de Breaute, a famous mercenary. Sir Walter's daughter married Sir Geoffrey Gascelyn and it was he who had the porch built, which of course is now 700 years old. In 1424 the manor was sold to the Hungerford family who held it for 260 years. Then the estate was again sold and passed through various hands until it was bought by the present family in 1917. Since 1424 the house has been continuously occupied and the names of all the occupants are recorded.

Originally there was a village to the west of the house. In 1282 it had thirteen cottages and the list of rents and services payable to the lord of the manor still exists; possibly this document is unique. By 1582 the village had disappeared. The house, which is still a family home, is open to the public.

Not far away, on the lane to Biddestone, is Starveall Farm. In this lovely old farmhouse there are two potters at work and a wide range of pots is on sale, along with naturally dyed woollen items and herbs.

Travel out to **Biddestone** where one may feed the ducks on the pond and admire the lovely old houses which spread around the green. Also by the quiet back lanes Castle Combe can be found.

Castle Combe has become world famous as the prettiest village in England and certainly the grouping of church, cottages and old covered market, against a backdrop of trees, makes a very pretty picture. A favourite occupation seems to be spotting trout from the bridge over the stream, from where the best view may be obtained. The local museum includes finds from a nearby Roman villa.

Corsham is on the A4 between Chippenham and Bath. There was a settlement here before the Romans came. From humble beginnings, it grew to be a bustling weaving and market town with some delightful old buildings to admire. At the eastern end of the High Street, near Corsham Court, is a line of weavers' cottages. At the opposite end of the High Street and just a little way down at the junction of the Melksham and Lacock roads, are almshouses that were endowed and built in 1668 by Dame Margaret Hungerford, who was Lady of the Manor at that time.

Corsham Court is signposted off the A4. It was a royal manor in the days of the Saxon kings; the present house dates from 1582 and is now the home of Lord Methuen, whose family bought it to house a collection of sixteenth- and seventeenth-century Italian and Flemish paintings. This collection was added to in the nineteenth century when more paintings were brought in. Though still the home of the Methuen family, the house is open to the public and contains other treasures in addition to the magnificent collection of pictures. The gardens, which are open, were originally laid out by Capability Brown in 1760 but later completed by Humphrey Repton. Though worth visiting at any time of the year, spring is perhaps the best time, when the magnolias and daffodils appear. There is an intriguing Gothic Bath House in the grounds and peacocks strut around, sometimes even down the High Street, where the locals are so used to them they hardly take notice.

Outside the main gardens stands the church of St Bartholomew. It contains features of the original Saxon church which was mentioned in the Domesday Book. The church was rebuilt in the twelfth century and later centuries saw many other changes. There are

Castle Combe

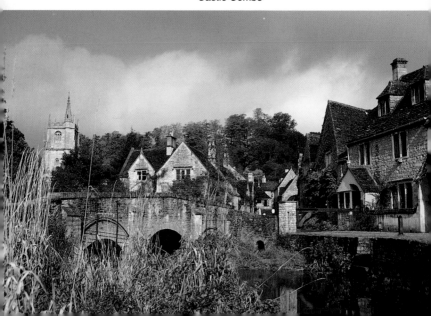

Great Chalfield Manor House

The Courts garden at Holt, near Bradford-on-Avon

many fascinating features and students of such matters will find an explanatory leaflet available giving details of the history of the changes.

Beyond the church it is possible to walk along the paths of the park and see the 13-acre lake, also planned by Capability Brown but completed by Repton 40 years later, a haven of peace in a lovely rural setting.

Box village lies halfway between Chippenham and Bath, 'The last village in Wiltshire on the road to Bath'. It was popular in Roman times and there are remains of villas in the area. Bath stone was quarried extensively from the area just to the east and is still extracted in the district.

Brunel's famous Box tunnel is its present-day claim to fame and in 1987 the west portal of the tunnel was cleaned and restored; it can be viewed from the A4 where a plaque has been erected to commemorate the fact. The tunnel is 2,947m (3,212yd) long, and when it was built it was the longest railway tunnel in the world. It has been said that the alignment of the tunnel is such that the sun shines through on 9 April, Brunel's birthday, but many locals believe that it is the midsummer sunrise that can be seen.

One mile south-east from Box, at **Chapel Plaister** there is a tiny wayside chapel, which was built in the fifteenth century as a hospice and church for pilgrims on the way to Glastonbury. The pilgrims' symbol of a cockle shell is above the door. The chapel is easy to miss as it stands at the top of the hill among a group of stone buildings.

Still going south-east, the manor house of **Great Chalfield** must be carefully sought out by the discerning visitor. It lies between the B3109 and the B3107, 2 miles from Bradford-on-Avon, close to Holt, and must be reached by narrow lanes. It was built about 1480 by Thomas Tropenell and may be considered as one of the most important Tudor manor houses in the country. Water from the nearby stream feeds the moat round this National Trust property which was originally walled but now only the remains show along the edge of the moat. It was built of local stone which mellows beautifully and is a considerable part of the charm of this lovely house. The dining room holds a portrait of the builder and there is also a great hall. The church is thirteenth century but was added to by Thomas Tropenell, who gave it the bell tower and spire. The gardens of the manor house are also open to the public and the grouping of house and garden, with the church (also entered via the entrance drive to the house) is especially pleasing.

Not far away, at **Holt**, is The Courts, which is also a National Trust property, but only the gardens are open. Originally The Courts was the place where weavers brought their disputes until the end of the eighteenth century. There are over 3 acres of formal gardens divided by yew hedges. This area includes a lily pond and herbaceous borders. Another area of over 3 acres is dedicated to wild flowers and an arboretum.

Bradford-on-Avon now lies only 2 miles to the west and there are more treasures there to be seen. In this ancient town, which is mentioned in the Domesday Book, history spans the centuries. It has the most complete Saxon church in England, a Norman church, a Tudor mansion, a tithe barn, a lock-up and much more. The gem is the Saxon church dedicated to St Lawrence which is believed to have been built by St Aldhelm. For centuries it was lost, until in 1858 the vicar of Bradford, looking down from the hill, noticed the grouping of buildings round what appeared to be a church. Research showed that the chronicler William of Malmesbury had recorded a church there. At the time when the vicar first noticed the church, the chancel had been made into a two storey cottage and the nave was a school with the schoolmaster's house built up against it, also a wool factory butted onto the west wall. The church had been 'lost' for 150 years. At one time it was mentioned in a deed as the Skull House, into which dead men's bones were thrown. It was not until 1870 that the various additional buildings were removed and the church restored. Professor Freeman went to see it and declared it to be the most untouched example of the seventh century, but it was later declared to be eleventh century. However, it is beautiful in its stark bare simplicity. It is a high, narrow building with the narrowest chancel arch in England at just over a metre wide.

Across the road is the 'modern' church, the one the Normans built. It was restored in the last century, a period when many of the churches in Britain were saved from falling to pieces. The church has some fine memorials. One is to Thomas Horton and his wife, who brought prosperity to the town in the fifteenth century with the wool trade. Another memorial is to the Shrapnel family who lived in Bradford for three generations. It was Lieutenant General Henry Shrapnel who invented the Shrapnel shell in 1785, a shell which it is claimed won many victories.

There are many other interesting buildings in the town, all in mellow honey-coloured Bath stone. The chantry by the church is fifteenth century; Lord Methuen's ancestors lived at The Priory for a hundred years; Westbury House is a handsome building, outside which a mob gathered in 1791 to protest about machinery being

Bradford-on-Avon

Church Street, Bradford-on-Avon

introduced into a mill by the house owner. He gave the mob the machinery and they destroyed it by fire on the bridge.

The finest house in Bradford is The Hall which is a beautiful Elizabethan building, built by John Hall in 1610. Later it was used as a model for the British Pavilion at the Paris Exhibition in 1900. Only the grounds may be seen, by appointment.

The lofty beauty of The Hall is in complete contrast to The Shambles. This surviving medieval section is now a shopping area with antique shops, tea shops and many interesting buildings.

The bridge itself is a relic from the past. It was enlarged in the seventeenth century from the original thirteenth-century packhorse bridge, and the bridge chapel was rebuilt as a lock-up. It was here that John Wesley once spent an uncomfortable night in one of the two cells.

In the year 1001 Bradford was given to Shaftesbury Abbey and the town grew so rich that early in the fourteenth century a great tithe barn was built. It is one of the largest remaining tithe barns in England, being 50m (164ft) long and 10m (33ft) wide, with fourteen great bays and four projecting gabled porches. Some of the timber of the great doors is six hundred years old. The massive roof timbers bear an estimated 30,000 stone roof tiles weighing 100 tons. It is now the home of an agricultural museum and the blend of ancient building and old equipment is very fitting. The barn stands in meadows by the river and close by is a packhorse bridge as old as the barn.

The centrepiece of the local museum, in Bridge Street, is a pharmacist's shop which served the town for over 120 years.

The town was once the centre of the woollen industry and this was the source of its prosperity — the Yorkshire wool town of Bradford was named after it. There are many interesting buildings relating to the trade, particularly the large mills alongside the river, now given over to other uses, while up the hillside are rows of attractive eighteenth-century workers' cottages. This area is known as Tory, not from any political affiliation, but from being built on a tor, or high place.

Close by Bradford is the hamlet of **Westwood**. To find this village go south on the B3109, signposted to Frome, then turn west on a minor road. Westwood has both a fifteenth-century church and a manor. The church has a Georgian roof with fine plastered bosses, a Jacobean pulpit and some original fifteenth-century stained glass.

Next door to the church is Westwood Manor, a National Trust property. The stone manor house dates from late in the fifteenth century. It was altered in the early seventeenth century but retains late Gothic and Jacobean windows. The Great Hall dates from 1490 and the Great Parlour and Kings Room have fine seventeenth-century decorative plasterwork ceilings. This charming and unique house is set in a modern topiary garden.

Just a little further west is **Iford**, which also has a manor house and though it is not open to the public, the gardens are and they are quite famous. It is claimed that these gardens, laid out in Italian style, influenced Sir Edwin Lutyens and Gertrude Jekyll. They were laid out by the owner, the Edwardian landscape architect, Harold Peto. In this beautiful and idyllic valley of the River Frome the gardens rise steeply up the hillside behind the Tudor manor house. The house fronts onto the river near an ancient bridge while to the rear of the house, the terraces rise up to beech woods on the ridge. This romantic garden contains pools and summer houses, a colonnade and a cloister, antique statues and many interesting plants.

By returning to Westwood and continuing along the minor road one may arrive at **Trowbridge**, now the county administrative centre and a bustling small town. Originally it was one of the weaving towns and is mentioned in the Domesday Book, the town developing around the castle of the de Bohuns. Fore Street curves around in an approximation of the line of the walls. The church was begun in the thirteenth century but was rebuilt in the fifteenth century and again in the nineteenth, but on the fifteenth-century plan. It is claimed that the spire is the best of any parish church in Wiltshire. In the churchyard is the tomb of Thomas Helliber, hanged on his nineteenth birthday, 22 March 1803, as one of the ringleaders of the rioting which took place over the introduction of machinery into the weaving industry. To the last he claimed his innocence. In The Parade there are still some eighteenth-century houses to be seen. A famous son of Trowbridge was Sir Isaac Pitman, the inventor of a shorthand system. There is a plaque, a bust in the town hall and Pitman Avenue to commemorate him. The poet George Crabbe was rector here from 1814 to 1832.

Trowbridge Museum, in the civic hall, tells the story of this woollen town with working textile machinery, children's toys and games from the eighteenth century, and also household objects.

Lovers of churches will want to visit **Steeple Ashton** where the lovely church is a fine example of fifteenth-century Perpendicular architecture. There are many interesting features about the church, but the village itself is also interesting. The cross on the green was set on stones already there when the Normans arrived. It was itself erected in 1071 though repaired in 1714. At the top are four sundials, a ball, a cross and a crown. The adjacent lock-up is traditional, with a domed roof and no windows. There are some lovely old houses set round the green and on down the long main street, of herringbone pattern red brick, and half timbered.

Not far south-east is **Edington Priory**, founded in 1362 by William of Edington, Lord Chancellor of England and Bishop of Winchester. This beautiful building is now the parish church and is famous for its music festivals. There are many fine features including a fourteenth-century Madonna and glass from the same era. In the fifteenth century the Bishop of Salisbury, the Venerable William Ayscough, fled to Edington to escape the violence at Salisbury during Jack Cade's rebellion. During High Mass he was dragged from the church 'to the top of the hill' and there brutally murdered.

Edington is on the B3098. To the west is **Bratton** and above the village is Bratton Castle, an ancient earthwork that is said to have been used as a shelter by the Danes as they retreated after being defeated by King Alfred. It covers 23 acres and has a double row of ramparts. The views are magnificent and it is a favourite place for kite flying or just strolling round. There is a topograph so one may enjoy trying to spot some of the places indicated. The white horse cut into the hill just below the castle is probably the oldest in Wiltshire, possibly as old as the adjacent Berkshire white horse. It is believed to celebrate Alfred's victory over the Danes, though it was remodelled in 1778.

A short run from here is **Westbury**. The parish church here is built on foundations 1,000 years old but most that can be seen is about 700 years old. In the old market place there are some interesting buildings including the fourteenth-century Lopes Arms and the town hall built in 1815. Westbury has restored the old Victorian swimming pool and opened it for use, the only one of its kind still open for swimming.

A trip with a difference from Westbury is round the Blue Circle Cement Works, by prior arrangement only, but quite interesting. The company unobtrusively quarry quite close to Bratton Castle but there is no road traffic. The chalk is moved to the works as a slurry down a pipeline, nothing being visible to the observer from the valley except the tall chimney, which is a landmark for miles around. There is a constant plume of steam from its top by which means it can be pinpointed from a great distance away.

Nearby **Old Dilton** church is a fine example of a thirteenth-century church and just across the A3098 is Chalcot House, a small

Iford Manor and the bridge over the River Frome

Steeple Ashton

Palladian manor house. It was once derelict, but has been restored and saved from complete destruction.

Two miles north (though there is no direct main road) is the **Brokerswood Woodland Park**. Here there are 8 acres of broad leaf woodland. There are nature trails of varying length, a picnic area, children's adventure playground and a woodland museum. The Woodland Heritage Museum houses displays on wildlife and birds, conservation, natural history and forestry. There is a varied programme of special events including craft fairs and children's days.

Camping and caravanning is available at the Woodland Park and the site is very well equipped. There is also coarse fishing on the lake.

Additional Information

Accommodation

£££ = expensive
££ = moderate
£ = inexpensive
EM = evening meal available

Calne

*Lansdowne Strand Hotel
& Restaurant* (££, EM)
The Strand, SN11 0JR
☎ 01249 8124988

Mrs Sinden (£, EM)
Lowbridge Farm, Bremhill, SN11 9HE
☎ 01249 815889

Wayside (£, EM)
Chittoe Heath, Bromham SN15 2EH
☎ 01380 850458

Corsham

Mr & Mrs Smith (£)
Home Farm, Biddestone, Corsham,
SN14 7DQ
☎ 01249 714475
Food nearby.

The Methuen Arms Hotel (£££, EM)
2 High Street, SN13 0HB
☎ 01249 714867

Melksham

Conigre Farm Hotel (£££, EM)
Semington Road, SN12 6BZ
☎01225 702229

The Kings Arms Hotel (££, EM)
Market Place, SN12 6EX
☎ 01225 707272

Mrs Mc'Dowell (££)
Lacock Pottery, The Tan Yard,
Lacock, SN15 2LB
☎ 01249 730266. Food nearby.

Trowbridge

Old Manor Hotel (£££, EM)
Trowle, BA14 9BL
☎ 01225 777393

Hilbury Court Hotel (££)
Hilperton Road, BA14 7JW
☎ 01225 752949

Places to Visit

Bradford-on-Avon

Bradford on Avon Museum
Bridge Street, BA15 1BY
☎ 01225 863280
Open: Easter-October Wednesday-
Saturday 10.30am-12.30pm, 2-4pm,
Sunday 2-4pm; November-Easter
Wednesday-Sunday 2-4pm,
Saturday 10.30am-12.30pm, 2-4pm.
Admission free.

The Courts (NT)
Holt, BA14 6RR
☎ 01225 782340
Garden open: April-October
Sunday-Friday 2-5pm.

Great Chalfield Manor (NT)
Near Holt, SN12 8NJ
☎ 01985 843600
Open: April-October Tuesday-
Thursday, guided tours at 12.15,
2.15, 3, 3.45 and 4.30pm. Closed
public holidays.

Iford Manor Gardens
Westwood
☎ 01225 863146
Open: May-September daily except
Monday and Friday, 2-5pm; April
& October Sundays and Easter, 2-
5pm.

Tithe Barn
☎ 01272 750700 for opening times

Westwood Manor (NT)
Westwood, BA15 2AF
☎ 01225 863374
Open: April-October, Sunday,
Tuesday and Wednesday, 2-5pm.
Other times by written appointment.

Castle Combe
Museum
The Hill, SN14 7HU
☎ 01249 782250
Open: Easter-October Sunday 2-5pm, or by appointment. Admission free.

Calne
Bowood House & Gardens
☎ 01249 812102
Open: April-October 11am-6pm (or dusk if earlier).

Chippenham
Chippenham Yelde Hall Museum
Market Place SN15 3HL
☎ 01249 651488
Open: mid-March to October, Monday-Saturday 10am-12.30pm, 2-4.30pm. Closed Bank Holidays. Free admission.

Lackham Country Attractions
Lackham College, nr Lacock, SN15 2NY
☎ (01249) 443111
Open: Easter-October daily, 11am-5pm.

Sheldon Manor
House open: Thursday, Sunday and Bank Holiday Mondays, 2-6pm.
Garden open: 12.30-6pm.

Corsham
Corsham Court
☎ 01249 701610/701611
Open: daily except Monday & Friday, January to November, 2-4.30pm; Easter to September 2-6pm, including Friday and Bank Holidays. Other times by appointment.

Lacock
Lacock Abbey (NT)
☎ 0249 73227
Abbey open: April-October daily except Tuesday 1-5pm, closed Good Friday.
Grounds and cloisters open: April-October daily except Tuesdays 12 noon-5.30pm, closed Good Friday.
Fox Talbot Museum open: April-October daily 11am-5.30pm, closed Good Friday.

Trowbridge
Trowbridge Museum
The Shires, Court Street, BA14 8AT
☎ 01225 751339
Open: Tuesday-Friday 12 noon-4pm (10am-4pm school holidays), Saturday 1am-5pm. Admission free.

Tourist Information Centres

Bradford-on-Avon
☎ 01221 65797

Melksham
☎ 01225 707424

Trowbridge
☎ 01225 777054

Westbury
☎ 01373 827158

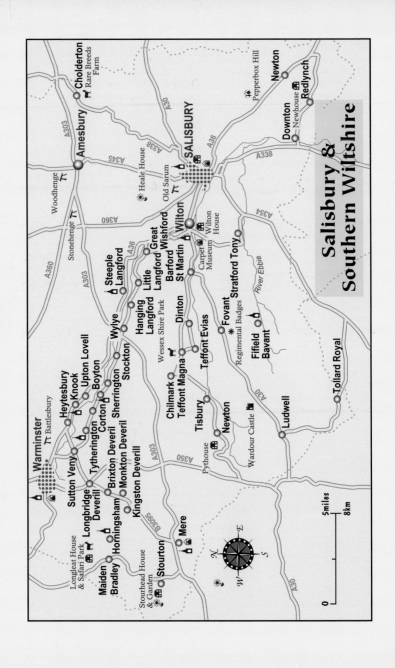

Salisbury & Southern Wiltshire

Salisbury & Southern Wiltshire

11

From Westbury it is only about 4 miles to Warminster by the A350. However, a watershed has been crossed. The streams around Westbury run into the Bristol Avon, while those around Warminster run into the Hampshire Avon, though the latter rises in Wiltshire.

The Downs around **Warminster** abound with traces of Bronze and Iron Age remains. Battlesbury Camp, quite close to town, is one of Britain's major Iron Age forts. Finds of large numbers of skeletons at Battlesbury seem to indicate tribal warfare.

There was a thriving agricultural community here when the Romans came, though there was no town then. It was a royal manor in the time of King Alfred and later, about AD978, coins were minted, which probably ensured the success of the town as a market place. Coins were still minted occasionally until about AD1135.

The arrival of the Normans seems to have made little difference.

above: Longleat House

The royal manor had been held by Edward the Confessor and passed instead to King William. In 1156 the manor was sold by the Crown to one Robert Maudit. His family held it until the sixteenth century when it was bought by the Thynne family of Longleat. The Marquess of Bath is still the lord of the manor.

Warminster's mellowed streets have many buildings of interest including inns, surviving from the days when the town was a coaching centre. The greatest building is the Parish Church of St Denys. Sometimes called The Minster, it is a fourteenth-century building with some Norman work. The tower is fifteenth century and survived rebuilding programmes in the eighteenth and nineteenth centuries. There are several other churches in the town but the main interest is the historic Chapel of St Lawrence. It was built in the early thirteenth century but only the fourteenth-century tower has survived intact, though there are interesting carvings and gargoyles in the building. The chapel is unusual in that the administration is neither lay nor ecclesiastical but 'Twelve, Ten or Eight of the principal, honest and discreet men of the parish of Warminster'.

The Dewey Museum is housed in the local library, which is just off the Three Horse Shoes shopping mall in the town centre. Also in the town centre are the Old Bell Hotel, a fourteenth-century coaching inn, and The Bath Arms, an eighteenth-century coaching inn. A prominent building is the town hall which was built in 1830 by Sir Edward Blore. It belonged to the Marquess of Bath and was given to the town in 1904; it now belongs to the county council and is used as a magistrates court. Across the road is Dewey House (also designed by Sir Edward Blore), now the home of the town council.

The Lake Pleasure Grounds are one of the town's pleasing features. Just off Weymouth Street and close to the town centre, the gardens lie in the sheltered valley of the River Were. Smooth lawns and flower beds are sheltered by green slopes on either side. The stream feeds a large boating lake and there are tennis courts, a putting green and children's corner, which has a paddling pool and an adventure playground.

On Arn hill to the north of the town is a fine eighteen-hole golf course with superb views. Close by is Copheap, a high, steep hill. A lych gate and a 'Path of Remembrance' lead from the town to the beech woods. It makes a most attractive walk from the town.

Nearby are the famous Lions of Longleat. **Longleat**, of course, is much more than just a huge, splendid safari park. At first it was a monastic house but after the dissolution it was purchased by Sir John Thynne in 1540. He did a lot of building but sadly his efforts burnt down in 1567. However, he began again and the resultant early Renaissance-style house has remained in the same family, almost unchanged, for the last four hundred years. The fourth marquess returned from the Grand Tour with new ideas and set about embellishing his home in the Italian style. In many rooms there are unique Venetian ceilings and decorations. There are also tapestries and wall hangings, paintings, furniture and table settings, which include the State Dining Room table laden with silver. This great house is indeed memorable.

In addition there are the Victorian kitchens, nineteenth-century dolls' houses, a pets' corner and various exhibitions. There is a maze, a garden centre and safari boat rides on a lake inhabited by sea lions and hippopotomi. An island on the lake is home to families of gorilla and chimpanzee.

Then of course, there is the safari park itself, a drive through lions, baboons, zebra, giraffe etc, though not all at the same time.

To the south, at the end of a drive almost a mile long, is **Horn-ingsham**. In this straggling village is the oldest nonconformist chapel in England, reputedly founded in 1566 by Sir John Thynne as a place of worship for a company of Scottish artisans, brought down to work on the big house. There was nowhere else at that time so Sir John had the chapel built for them. They lived on the edge of the village in 'Little Scotland' and Scotland still features on detailed maps. The chapel was rebuilt in 1700.

Take the minor road to Maiden Bradley then the B3092 towards Mere. On the way are **Stourhead House and Gardens**. The gardens are said to be as fine as any in Europe. **Stourton** village belonged to the Stourton family for generations, from Saxon times, until the Hoare family came in 1717 and the banker, Henry Hoare, purchased the estate. Stourhead House was built by the Hoare family in 1722 and later enlarged. In 1902 a fire damaged the central part of the house but it was rebuilt by Sir Henry, the last baron to live at the house. His son died in World War I and the house and estate were given to the National Trust in 1946. A member of the family still lives close by. This elegant Palladian house contains original Chip-pendale furniture and fine paintings.

Lakes and temples set in woodland, with tulip trees, beech trees, rhododendrons and many rare varieties make the gardens beautiful almost any time of year. The Bristol Cross is perhaps the most curious object to be seen. This lovely carved cross was first set up in the streets of Bristol in 1373 and was heightened and repaired after three hundred years. In 1737 it was thought to be in the way and

Stourhead House and Gardens

moved to College Green. It stayed there for only 30 years, after which it was taken down and stored in the cathedral. The citizens of Bristol regarded the cross as 'a public nuisance' and 'a ruinous and superstitious relick'. In 1764, after only 2 years in the cathedral, the pieces were given to Henry Hoare. It took six wagons to haul them to Stourton, where they were put back together.

The nearby 'Turf Bridge' was designed by Henry after the style of the Palladios Bridge at Vicenze.

The village church of Stourton is mainly late medieval. There are some fragments of ancient glass and memorials to the Hoare family and to the earlier Stourton family. Adjacent to the church is a line of old cottages and a little higher up the road is the Spread Eagle Inn, which offers the usual refreshments and accommodation.

On the Stourton estate is the Neolithic causewayed camp of White Sheet Hill and a group of bowl barrows. A path goes from near the village, across the B3092, easterly up the 2 miles to the hill. There are magnificent views south and west into Dorset and Somerset.

On the edge of the Stourhead estate, but 3½ miles from the house by road, is King Alfred's Tower, a 160ft high brick folly built in 1772, giving fine views over Somerset, Dorest and Wiltshire.

Follow the B3092 into **Mere**. The town gets its name from John Mere whose badge was a sailing ship, and from this derives the Ship Inn. John Mere founded a chantry in the church in the fourteenth century. The house which is now the Ship Inn was built in the seventeenth century by Sir John Coventry, who was 'sent to Coventry' or banished by the king because of some rude remarks. The diarist Samuel Pepys mentions the loud mouthed knight. At the other inn in the village, The Talbot, Charles II dined after escaping from Worcester. It is known that he slept at Zeals House, not far away.

William Barnes, the Dorset dialect poet, lived at the house called The Chantry and kept a small school. The gardens slope down to a stream which escapes through a wall. There is a poem which William Barnes left in farewell to this garden when he moved to Dorchester to find a better place for his school:

'Sweet garden! Peaceful spot! No more in thee
Shall I e'er while away the sunny hour …'

The parish church has a splendid Perpendicular tower, more typical of the great towers in Somerset. From the old castle hill one may see the three counties of Wiltshire, Somerset and Dorset. There is a small local history museum (situated in the library) which is made up of display cases. There is also a small museum in the church tower which is open by appointment only. Now the A303 bypasses the town it is pleasantly peaceful.

Head in a north-easterly direction on the B3095 along a pleasing rural vale, the Deverill Valley. The road climbs up over the Downs and descends along the infant River Wylye through the five Deverill villages. In order of descent down the valley they are: Kingston Deverill, Monkton Deverill, Brixton Deverill, Hill Deverill and finally Longbridge Deverill.

Kingston Deverill has a great heap of sarsen stones (now in the grounds of the holiday apartment house), believed to have been the spot where King Alfred met the converging forces of Somerset, Hampshire and Wiltshire on his march against the Danes.

Longbridge Deverill has a group of charming almshouses built in 1665 by the Lord of Longleat, Sir James Thynne. They are near the early Norman church which is the resting place of Sir John Thynne, the builder of Longleat, who died in 1580. This last Deverill village lies on the A350. Cross the main road and proceed down the Wylye valley still on the B3095. At the first crossroads turn right through the long straggling village of **Sutton Veny**. The road now roughly runs parallel to the A36 Warminster to Salisbury road through some of the lovely old Wiltshire countryside as it goes down the Wylye valley to Wilton. This is a pleasant route to meander along, through water meadows with the wooded downland slopes looking down on either side. Almost at the end of the village there is a narrow lane to the left. This leads down to a lovely old church, partly in ruins but with the chancel remaining. This church, dedicated to St Leonard, is in the care of the Redundant Churches Fund.

At **Tytherington** there is a small church which has stood there on its grassy knoll since 1083. It is believed to be the oldest church in Wiltshire. Empress Mathilda endowed this simple place in 1140. The side road here leads across the river to **Heytesbury**. The village had a bypass built in 1986 so the main street has returned to the relative tranquillity it used to know. This was another of the manors owned by the powerful Hungerford family. In the fourteenth century, Walter Hungerford founded the almshouses, which still exist. They burned down in 1770 but were rebuilt. In the village street there is an old stone lock-up and The Angel Inn, a thirteenth-century coaching house that still offers hospitality. In the centre of the village is the impressive church of St Peter and St Paul which has a thirteenth-century tower with a medieval bell. It is possible to take a lovely riverside walk to **Knook** to visit another tiny church which some believe to be Saxon, though learned authorities claim it is

Norman. The remnants of a once thriving monastery and village now lie very peacefully, close to the river where the road ends.

Upton Lovell, Corton and Boyton lie on the way downstream to Sherrington. Here, in the days of the Plantagenets, there was a castle which was the home of the Giffards of Boyton. In the church at **Boyton** there is a chantry chapel built in 1266 by Godfrey, Bishop of Worcester and Lord Chancellor of England. A headless skeleton found in a tomb in the church is thought to be that of John Gifford, who was executed in 1322 for taking part in an uprising led by Thomas Plantagenet. The best way to see **Sherrington** is to walk round the loop of road off the main valley road. At the lower end of the village near the river there used to be watercress beds made by creating a large pond, but they are no longer in production.

Stockton's buildings include thatched cottages, Victorian school, almshouses and a fine church, the latter being part-medieval and part-Norman. There are two interesting tombs, one to a governor of the Gold Coast who returned to become a commissioner of the navy, and another to a lady's maid, Anne Roxworthy, who retired to live nearby. Anne felt she had become too proud so she asked to be buried in the porch, where everyone could walk over her.

Wylye is next; another village saved from the curse of traffic by a bypass (the A303 used to use the village street). The River Wylye runs quietly under the old bridge, past the old mill. It has a quaint old street called Teapot Street and another called Sheepwash Lane.

Hanging Langford lies peacefully on the minor road while **Steeple Langford** straddles stream-filled meadows and, unfortunately, the A36. The interesting church has work from all the centuries, from the twelfth-century font up to the seventeenth-century pulpit. Henry Collier was rector here at one time and two of his sons fought in the Penruddock Rebellion. When caught, they were sent to Jamaica and sold as slaves. **Little Langford** has a tiny church down a side lane, over the railway.

Great Wishford, a gentle village, lies in a bend of the river, neither on the A36 nor on the minor road, but in between. In the churchyard wall is a price of bread memorial, giving bread prices in 1800, 1801, 1904, 1920, 1946, 1965 and 1971. An oak tree stands in the village, under which the Wishford Oak Apple Club used to hold meetings, and the village still remembers the festival. It is believed to stem from pagan tree worship. The call 'Grovely! Grovely!' is raised as oak boughs are laid before the church altar, an old custom celebrating the rights of villagers to gather wood in Grovely Woods. In 1603 the right was conferred on villagers for all time.

♣ **Grovely Wood** is the great stretch of woodland topping the Downs to the south. The wood is still over 5 miles long and 2 miles wide in some places. In the thirteenth-century church dedicated to St Michael is a memorial to Sir Richard Grobsham, lord of the manor in the sixteenth century. He killed a wild boar in Grovely Wood and is said to be the last man to do so. Sir Richard's feet lie on a carved boar's head under a canopy which counts among one of the county's finest seventeenth-century monuments. Grovely Wood was once one of the largest woods in Wiltshire and there are the remains of a British camp a mile long in the wood. The Roman road from Old Sarum to the lead mines on the Mendips goes through the middle and the route can still be walked in the woods as it is mostly bridleway. From Wishford it is a little over 2 miles to Wilton.

Using Wilton as a base there is another fascinating valley to explore, the valley of the River Nadder. Take the A30 Shaftesbury Road and at the village of Barford St Martin go onto the B3089 to **Dinton**. The old part of the village is on the road north past the church. The National Trust owns four houses here. The largest is Philipps House, an imposing mansion in the neo-classical style and built in Chilmark stone, completed in 1816 and replacing an earlier house. It is let to the YWCA and can only be visited by written

The old church, Sutton Veny

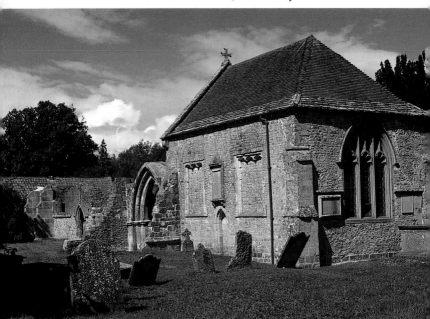

Wylye

appointment. Two other Trust properties in the villages are Hydes House and Lawes Cottage, a seventeenth-century stone building, once the home of William Lawes the composer. Neither of these are open. The remaining property is Little Clarendon, a stone Tudor house which is late fifteenth century, open by written appointment.

The villages of **Teffont Evias** and **Teffont Magna** are charming and unspoilt, with a small stream splashing down under little stone bridges into the lake by the manor before joining the Nadder.

At Teffont Magna is the 130-acre Wessex Shire Park and Country Centre, with a glorious panorama of Wiltshire's unspoilt countryside. There are walks and trails through bluebell and rhododendron woods. The centre is worked with crops being harvested by horse power and the horses graze free in the meadows. Apart from the shire horses, there are other animals, special breeds, a children's animal encounter area, a working blacksmith's forge and a display of historic farm machinery. There are also free horse-drawn cart rides, a children's play area, a picnic area and a restaurant.

Go by way of **Chilmark**, of the famous Chilmark stone, which is a fine creamy limestone. The quarries have been used since Roman times and many fine examples of the stone may be seen in the county and indeed countrywide. A fourteenth-century mathematician and philosopher, John de Chilmark, may have been baptised in the church. He was called the Archimedes of his age. People from Chilmark sailed in the Mayflower and there is a Chilmark in Massachusetts where they settled.

Follow the lanes to **Tisbury**. This is one of Wiltshire's oldest towns and it has one of England's biggest barns. This huge tithe barn is at Place Farm. It has 500sq m (5,400sq ft) of thatch and is over 60m (200ft) long. There are some lovely old buildings in the main street of Tisbury and at the bottom, by the river, is the lovely church of St John the Baptist. In the graveyard, Rudyard Kipling's parents are buried. There is a memorial recording the early days of colonisation in America. Ann, third daughter of Baron Arundell's second wife, married Lord Baltimore. He was granted a charter to settle what is now Maryland, named after King Charles' Queen, Henrietta Maria. There is an Arundell County in Maryland and in Massachusetts there is a Tisbury and also East and West Tisburys.

Lady Blanche is buried at Tisbury. She defended Wardour Castle for the king in the Civil War. With only a handful of men she held out against a force of over a thousand, led by Sir Edward Hungerford. After a siege the castle was surrendered and despite promises, the place was looted. Lady Blanche, who was at that time about sixty, was sent as a prisoner to Shaftesbury. After her release she lived at Winchester. He ghost is said to walk the castle grounds.

Wardour Castle lies some 2 miles south-west of Tisbury. This castle, begun in 1393, is unique in England. To find anything similar one must go to France, to the Château de Concressault. Not a fortress in the usual 'castle' sense, it was built as a tower house with provision for some defensive capability. What makes Wardour unique is its hexagonal shape. Within is a hexagonal courtyard and there is sufficient of the building left for the imagination to be able to fill in some gaps. There is a small lake in front of the castle and a Gothic pavilion bonded to the outer bailey wall. The outer bailey is large and the wall is mostly intact for all its length. With the bailey is a small grotto. The whole aspect is pleasing, as the castle sits in a fold of the hills with woods all round.

Just over a mile away, near the village of **Newton**, is the Pythouse, built on similar lines to Philipps House but a little older. It is now mostly private apartments but the main reception and staircase may be viewed.

Go south on minor roads to cross the A30 at Ludwell, then take the minor road south which climbs the Downs. At the top turn left on a track to a car park. Here is **Win Green**, which is Wiltshire's highest point. There is a triangulation point and a clump of trees and very extensive views. It is supposedly possible to see the Isle of Wight and the Quantock Hills from here, but one would need a clear day. The National Trust own 38 acres of the hill which includes about three quarters of a mile of an ancient ridgeway track known as the Ox Drove. It is on the northern edge of Cranborne Chase which crosses the Dorset-Wiltshire border. The valley running south down to Tollard Royal is a haven of peace and quiet. A footpath goes down Ashcombe Bottom to **Tollard Royal**, royal because King John had a hunting lodge here. However, it is famous because of General Pitt-Rivers who was in the Crimean War. On his return he began excavations in the area and amassed a great and important collection of relics from the Stone Age and the Bronze and Iron Ages. One of his most important finds was a Saxon burial ground. There was a local museum for many years at Farnham, just over the Dorset border, but sadly it had to close. The exhibits were removed to Salisbury Museum. Many exhibits were already in Oxford Museum — there were so many finds that the small local museum could not house them all.

Return to the A30 and turn east. This is an interesting route and not too busy as the A303 takes a lot more traffic. To the south of the road near Fovant are regimental badges in the turf, cut by soldiers from Australia in World War I. The area was extensively used for training during that period.

Over the Downs, almost due south, is one of England's smallest churches, St Martin's church at **Fifield Bavant**, which is 10 by 5m (33 by 16ft). It has a thirteenth-century window and a Norman font. This southernmost valley in Wiltshire is quiet; the River Ebble runs its short length down here into the Avon south of Salisbury. At Stratford Tony turn north again, over the Downs, past Salisbury race course and down into Wilton.

Wilton is older than nearby Salisbury. It was once the capital of Wiltshire and of King Alfred's Wessex, with a nunnery and a royal palace here in Saxon times. After the dissolution, King Henry VIII gave the abbey, to William Herbert. Today it is still the family home of the Herbert family, the Earls of Pembroke.

Wilton House has seen many notable visitors in its time. Shakespeare himself, with his troupe, is said to have played *As you Like It* here for the first time, before King James I, in the Great Hall. Sir Phillip Sidney wrote the first part of *Arcadia* here and Charles I visited Wilton every year until the Civil War. The famous Double Cube room was the Operations Room for the top-secret planning by

Generals Eisenhower and Montgomery for the D-Day invasion of France. Winston Churchill painted here.

The house has eight superb seventeenth-century state rooms. Hans Holbein originally designed Wilton House, but a fire in 1647 destroyed most of it and it was rebuilt by Inigo Jones. Inside the collections are among the finest in Britain with paintings by Rubens, Rembrandt and Van Dyck. Other attractions include the Tudor kitchen, Victorian laundry, an historic tableau of dolls and toys through the ages, a teddy bear collection and a children's adventure playground. The grounds are a delight with fine mature trees, shrubs and flowers, and the lawns spread right down to the River Nadder which is spanned by a fine Palladian covered bridge.

Wilton is synonymous with carpets and here the world famous factory has its home. It is the oldest carpet factory in the world, being established on its present site in 1655. William III granted a charter to the company in 1699 and the regalia of the company is on display in the boardroom. The original carpets were not thought to be as good as the French-made ones and the then Earl of Pembroke smuggled two French weavers across the channel to train locals and to improve the Wilton weaving. There is a museum of carpet weaving and the modern factory may be visited. There is an audio-visual presentation, educational facilities, a weaver's shop and mill shop. Numbers may be limited in the factory for safety reasons and in busy times, so advance booking may be advisable.

Wilton has yet another claim to fame, the Parish Church of St Mary and St Nicholas. It was built between 1841 and 1845 in the style of the churches near Viterbo, north of Rome, and was one of the first churches to be built in England in the Lombardic style. The interior is very ornate with many ancient pieces incorporated, such as the four twisted columns studded with mosaic incorporated into the pulpit, which are of thirteenth-century origin. The marble columns at the east end came from a temple on the Gulf of Spezia which was built in 151BC. Surrounding the many wonders are the windows, which contain some priceless stained glass. Some of the glass is twelfth century, and there is glass from the thirteenth, fourteenth and fifteenth centuries. One window has glass dating from the fifteenth and sixteenth centuries which Napoleon took from Austria to Paris. Altogether it is a remarkable building.

Should you visit on a Sunday between Easter and the end of September, then a delightful tea may be taken in the tiny school room adjacent to the church. Local women put on a fine spread of home-made cakes, which are delicious.

The town centre has the old market square and the ruins of the medieval parish church of St Mary.

From Wilton take the Devizes road but at the junction with the A360 go straight ahead on a minor road which drops down into the lovely Woodford Valley. Heale House is about 4 miles from Wilton. The gardens are open and extend to about 8 acres beside the River Avon. There is a water garden surrounding a Japanese tea house and Nikki bridge, the whole surrounded by acers and magnolia, which make it particularly attractive in the spring. There is an interesting and varied collection of shrubs and plants, roses and clipped hedges. The sixteenth-century house is not open but it and its surroundings have changed little since Charles II sheltered here after the battle of Worcester in 1651.

By continuing the gentle meander up the valley the main A303 will be reached. Turn left then a right fork along the A344 leads, in less than a mile, to **Stonehenge**, the silent brooding monument high on the plain. Many books have been written supposedly explaining the site, but it keeps its secrets. To get a true perspective of Stonehenge one must walk along the 'old straight track' from Larkhill to the north, towards the stones, before the day's traffic has commenced. This outlines them on the horizon. The close up view of this

Stonehenge

unique monument, which is older than the pyramids, is awe inspiring.

Two miles to the east is the ancient town of **Amesbury**. There was a British camp here before the Romans came. The name of the town is said to derive from Amrosius who, in the fifth century, checked the Saxon invasion. There is a legend of perpetual choirs at Amesbury and a legend that Queen Guinevere founded a religious establishment here after the death of Arthur. On the death of Queen Guinevere, Sir Lancelot and his knights escorted her body back to Glastonbury to be buried with the king. In 980 Queen Elfrida founded a nunnery as a deed of atonement for the murder of her stepson, King Edward, at Corfe. The old church of St Mary and Melor was begun by the Saxons and refashioned by the Normans.

About 3½ miles to the east of Amesbury and just off the A303 is **Cholderton**. The Cholderton Rare Breeds Farm has all sorts of animals which we do not normally regard as endangered species, such as pigs, horses, sheep, rabbits and many more, but modern demands have left less requirement for some breeds. Also at the farm there are formal gardens and orchards, a woodland walk, a picnic site by a wildfowl pond and lunches or cream teas in the old flint farmhouse or on the terrace.

About a mile north is **Woodhenge** just by the slip road to Larkhill. This is one of the first major discoveries to have been made by aerial photography in Britain. It was photographed in 1925 by Squadron Leader Insall. It is not clear if it was a large circular building roofed in, or if it was open, as a wooden 'Stonehenge'. Within the inner ring was the grave of a child who had died from a cleft skull. The position is now marked with a cairn of stones. Dating has put the site at 2000BC. A hundred metres (330ft) north, and to be considered with Woodhenge, is the larger henge and timber circle known as Durrington Walls.

From this area the A345 leads south into Salisbury but on the way, to the north of Salisbury, is **Old Sarum**, an Iron Age hillfort. It was used by the Romans who called it *Sarviodunum*. A Saxon town stood here in the seventh century. A tenth-century brooch, coins and domestic objects found here may be seen in Salisbury museum. A mint was established here about 1004 during the reign of Ethelred. The Normans took over the huge defensive site and built a royal castle about 1068 and a cathedral in 1078. Stories are told about the move to the new town, including one of a shortage of water for the growing population, but in 1220 the bishop moved to the water meadows to the south and the new cathedral and its surrounding city began. The greater scope for expansion soon encouraged the population to follow and Old Sarum was slowly deserted.

Perhaps the first building in **Salisbury** was the church of St Thomas. It was built in 1220 for the workmen building the cathedral. The original wooden building was soon replaced with a stone building and this was rebuilt in the fifteenth century.

Salisbury has so many places of interest and is such a pleasant little city with a good selection of shops that to do the whole place justice would require a volume to itself. The information office has a newspaper-type publication for a modest charge which extensively covers the city and its surroundings. It lists restaurants and pubs, cafés and sports facilities. It gives the programme for the cinema, the playhouse and the arts centre as well as the diary of events through the whole year, which range from guided walks to Shakespeare at Wilton House, and from steam fairs to organ recitals in the cathedral.

The publication also has a circular walk round the city and one to Old Sarum with a detailed map and descriptions of places of interest. The points of interest in the city are numerous. The cathedral of course, with a video display in the cloisters and an original copy of the Magna Carta on display in the chapter house, one of only four made. There is a display, also in the cloisters, of the work involved in the continuing work of restoration. The interior of the cathedral is of magnificent. There is a medieval clock which was made in 1386 and is the oldest existing clock in England and probably the oldest in the world in working order. There is also a feature on brass rubbing and the opportunity to rub your own brass.

Round the cathedral close are grouped various museums. The Salisbury and South Wiltshire Museum, housed in the fourteenth-century Kings House, contains part of the Pitt-Rivers collection (the other part is in Oxford Museum), Early Man, the Stonehenge gallery and also a fine collection of Wedgwood and another of ceramics. The Wardrobe nearby is the military museum of the Royal Gloucestershire, Berkshire and Wiltshire Regiment. The story of the regiment is told with relics of their 250 years of proud service and with trophies and medals won. The thirteenth-century house is called the Wardrobe as, during the fourteenth century, the bishop used it as a store for his clothes.

Also in the close is Mompesson House (National Trust), a perfect early eighteenth-century town house. There is much eighteenth-century furniture and the collection of eighteenth-century drinking glasses has over 320 pieces. Of all the places of interest on the town

Salisbury Cathedral

Mompesson House, Cathedral Close, Salisbury

trail, none is later than fifteenth century except the College of Matrons which was founded in 1682.

Just along from the Close, near St Ann's Gate is Malmesbury House, a town house with fine rococo plasterwork that was visited by Charles II and the composer Handel; it is now open to the public.

Salisbury is not far from the borders with Dorset and Hampshire but there are two more places to visit. Pepperbox Hill on the A36 Southampton Road and Newhouse at Redlynch, just off the B3080, which leaves the A338 about 6 miles south of Salisbury at Downton.

At **Pepperbox Hill** the National Trust owns over 70 acres of open downland scattered with juniper bushes. There is a picnic site and the 'Pepperbox', which was built in 1606 by Giles Eyre, and given by the fifth Earl Nelson in 1949. This curious building may have been a folly or it may have been to allow the ladies to follow hunting or falconing from the top room. There is a green road running along the ridge eastwards towards Deanhill. A walk along here will be rewarding for the splendid views, over Salisbury to the north-east, and Southampton and the Isle of Wight in a southerly direction.

Go towards Southampton on the A36. In about a mile the A27 goes off to the east, but ignore that turn and in another mile at Newton turn right onto a minor road which meanders through to **Redlynch**. Here is Newhouse, a Jacobean brick-built 'Trinity' house with two Georgian wings dating from 1619. It contains a costume collection and a collection of Nelson relics.

Close by is **Downton**, a long, pleasant village. The old earthwork was a British fort taken over by the Saxons and used as a meeting place or 'moot'. The large church has some Norman work remaining in what is largely fourteenth and fifteenth century. The old manor house was once the home of the Raleigh family. Sir Walter Raleigh's brother Carew represented Downton in parliament.

Additional Information

Accommodation
££ = expensive
££ = moderate
£ = inexpensive
EM = evening meal available

Amesbury
Antrobus Arms Hotel (£££, EM)
15 Church Street, SP4 7EY
☎ 01980 623163

Fovant
Mrs P. Storey (££, EM)
Cross Keys, SP3 5JH
☎ 01722 714284

Salisbury
Mrs J. Bayley (££, EM)
Stratford Lodge, 4 Park Lane,
SP1 3NP
☎ 01722 325177

The Edwardian Lodge (££, EM)
59 Castle Road, SP1 3RH
☎ 01722 413329

The Millford Hall Hotel (££, EM)
206 Castle Street, SP1 3TG
☎ 01722 417411

Warminster
Old Bell Hotel (££, EM)
Market Place, BA12 9AN
☎ 01985 216611

Farmers Hotel (£, EM)
1 Silver Street, BA12 8PS
☎ 01985 213815

Wilton
Pembroke Arms Hotel (£££, EM)
Minister Street, SP2 0BH
☎ 01722 743328

Places to Visit

Amesbury
Cholderton Rare Breeds Farm Park
☎ 01980 629438
Open: daily Easter-October, 10am-
6pm (last admission 4.45pm).

Stonehenge
Open: daily April-May, September
to mid-October 9.30am-6pm; June
9.30am-7pm; July-August 9am-7pm;
mid-October-March 9.30am-4pm.

Mere
Mere Museum
Public Library, Barton Lane, BA12 6JA
Open: Monday & Friday 2-7.30pm,
Tuesday 10am-1pm and 2-5pm.
Also small museum in the church
tower open by appointment only
☎ 01747 860341

Newton
Pythouse
Near Wardour Castle
☎ 01747 870210

Open: May-September, Wednesday
and Thursday, 2-5pm, reception
and staircase only.

Redlynch
Newhouse
☎ 01725 20055
Open: Sunday and Bank Holiday
Mondays 2-5.30pm.

Salisbury
John Creasey Museum
Salisbury Library, Market Place
☎ 01722 324145
Open: Monday & Tuesday 10am-
5pm, Wednesday and Friday,
10am-7pm, Saturday 10am-4pm.
Admission free.

Heale Garden Plant Centre
Middle Woodford
Open: daily 10am-5pm.

Malmesbury House
St Ann's Gate, 15 The Close
☎ 01722 327027
Open: April-October, Tuesday,
Friday, Saturday & Bank Holiday
Monday 10am-5pm. Tours every
half hour.

Mompesson House (NT)
Cathedral Close, SP1 2EL
☎ 01722 335659
Open: April-October Saturday-
Wednesday 12 noon-5.30pm.

Old Sarum
Open: daily April-September 10am-
6pm, October-March 10am-4pm.

*Royal Gloucestershire, Berkshire &
   Wiltshire Regiment Museum*
The Wardrobe, 56 The Close
☎ 01722 414536
Open: 10am-4.30pm April-October
daily; November, February-March,
Monday-Friday.

Salisbury & South Wiltshire Museum
King's House, 65 The Close, SP1 2EN
☎ 01722 332151
Open: Monday-Saturday 10am-5pm.
Also Sunday in July & August 2-5pm.

Salisbury Cathedral
☎ 01722 328726
Open: daily May-August 8am-
8.15pm, September-April 8am-
6.30pm. Tours of the cathedral, tower
& workshops March-October;
evening tours of the cathedral &
tower May-August. Magna Carta on
view daily except December.

Stourton

Stourhead (NT)
☎ 01747 841152
House open: April-October
Saturday-Wednesday 12 noon-
5.30pm or dusk if earlier.
Gardens open: daily all year 9am-
7pm or sunset.
Refreshments and accommodation
at Spread Eagle Inn ☎ 01747 840587

King Alfred's Tower
☎ 01985 844785
Open: April-October, Tuesday-
Thursday 2-5.3pm, Saturday &
Sunday 10am-5.30pm or dusk if
earlier (open Good Friday & Bank
Holiday Monday).

Teffont Magna

Wessex Shire Park
Open: daily April-September
10am-6pm. Visitors welcome all
year but fewer facilities in winter.

Tisbury

Wardour Castle
Open: April-September daily 10am-
6pm, October daily 10am-4pm,
November-March Wednesday-
Sunday 10am-4pm.

Warminster

Dewey Museum
Public Library, Three Horseshoes
Mall, BA12 9BT
☎ 01985 216022
Open: Monday-Tuesday 10am-5pm,
Wednesday 10am-1pm, Thursday-
Friday 10am-7pm, Saturday 9am-
4pm. Closed Bank Holidays.

Longleat House & Safari Park
☎ 01985 844400
House open: Easter-September
10am-6pm; rest of the year 10am-
4pm. Closed 25 December.
Safari park open: mid-March to
October 10am-6pm, last admission
5.30pm or sunset if earlier.

Wilton

Wilton House
☎ 01722 743115
Open: Easter-October daily 11am-
6pm (last admission 5pm).

Wilton Carpet Factory & Museum
King Street, SP2 0AY
☎ 01722 744919/742733
Open: Monday-Saturday 9am-5pm,
Sunday 11am-5pm, except Bank
Holidays. Factory tours Monday-
Saturday 10.15am, 11.45am, 2pm,
3.30pm, Sunday 11.15am, 12.45pm,
2.30pm, 3.45pm.

Tourist Information Centres

Amesbury
☎ 01980 23255

Mere
☎ 01747 860341

Salisbury
Fish Row
☎ 01722 334956

Warminster
☎ 01985 218548

Somerset, Dorset & Wiltshire: Fact File

The information given here and in the Additional Information at the end of each chapter has been obtained from a number of sources. Admission charges have not been included as they are subject to revision.

Accommodation

A selected list is given at the end of each chapter. More detailed lists of all types of accommodation is available from Tourist Information Offices, while some can offer a booking service for a modest fee.

Archaeological & Historical Sites

All the sites listed below are open at any reasonable time, those with specified opening times are detailed in the Additional Information at the end of the appropriate chapter.

This part of Britain is rich in ancient remains. Wiltshire alone has more archaeological sites than any other area of comparable size in Europe, and there are also notable sites in the other two counties. This is a selection of the finest.

Avebury Stone Circle
Avebury.

Badbury Rings
Ancient hillfort at a Roman crossroads on the B3082 between Blandford Forum and Wimborne Minster.

Barbury Castle
Ancient hillfort south of Swindon.

Battlesbury Camp
Near Warminster.
Ancient causewayed camp.

Bratton Castle
Ancient hillfort near Westbury.

Brent Knoll
Ancient hill site, near the village of East Brent and Brent Knoll, just off the A370 near Burnham-on-Sea.

Burrow Mump
South of Bridgwater on the A361.
Ancient hill site, with an unfinished chapel on top.

Cadbury Castle
South of the A303 east of Wincanton, near the village of South Cadbury.
Supposed by some to be King Arthur's 'Camelot'.

Climate

Maximum and minimum daily temperatures

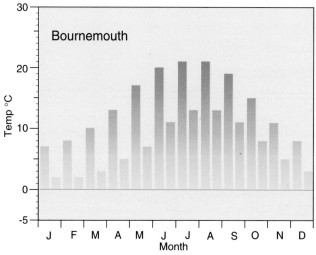

Average monthly rainfall

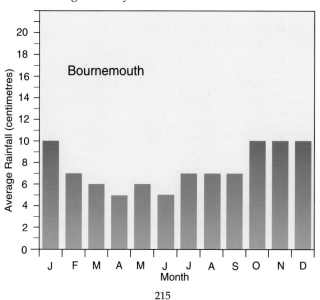

Cherhill Down
Ancient hillfort.

Knowlton Circles
Just off the B3078 Wimborne
Minster to Cranborne road.
Bronze Age henge and
ruined church.

Maiden Castle
Two miles south-west of
Dorchester.
A giant hillfort well pre-
served.

Maumbury Rings
Outskirts of Dorchester.
Prehistoric circle used by
the Romans as an amphi-
theatre and later for bear
baiting and executions.

Old Sarum
Original site of Salisbury.
1½ miles north of the city.

Silbury Hill
On the A4 near Avebury.
Largest prehistoric man-
made mound in Europe.

Stonehenge
Just west of Amesbury, at
the junction of the A303 and
the A344.

West Kennet Long Barrow
By the A4 just east of
Silbury Hill.
The largest chambered tomb
in England.

Woodhenge
On the A345 road, a mile
north of Amesbury.
A kind of Stonehenge
originally made of wood.

Country Parks

Castle Neroche
West of Ilminster, north of
the A303.
Country Park. Nature trail
and picnic site.

Coate Water
Swindon.
Woodland walks, Barbury
Castle, downland open
space.

Ham Hill
West of Yeovil, just off the
A3088.
Country park with exten-
sive views.

Penwood
South of Yeovil, south-west
from Sutton Bingham
reservoir.
Forest Park and nature trail.

Powerstock
North of Lyme Regis near
Wootton Fitzpaine.
Forest Park and forest trail,
picnic site.

Craft Workshops

There are so many rural craft workshops in the area, many of them reviving ancient crafts, that it is not possible to list them here. Local Information Offices have leaflets on a wide range of crafts from basket weaving to to winemaking and yarn spinning. Places where visitors may see items being made are listed in *Visiting Craft Workshops* (published by MPC).

Nature Reserves & Trails

Affpuddle Heath
South of the A31 near Tolpuddle.

Arne
Near Wareham.

Brean Down
Near Weston-Super-Mare. Part of Brean Down itself is a nature reserve.

Bridgwater
To the north at Steart Flats Nature reserve and bird sanctuary.

Brokerswood
Near Westbury Woodland museum.

Castle Neroche
On the Blackdown Hills.

Cloutsham
Exmoor.
Three miles through oak woods and over the moors.

Cotswold Water Park
Nature reserve and trails.

Cricklade
Ancient meadow.

Devizes, Roundway Down
Woodland nature trail.

Fyfield Down
Near Marlborough.
Open downland with sarsen stones.

Fyne Court
Visitor centre and nature reserve.

Minehead
North Hill, 3 miles.

Parks walk, ¾ mile on level, metalled path, following a stream from Parkhouse Road, near the town centre, to the western outskirts.

Nettlecombe Court
Brendon Hills.
Field study centre, open only by appointment.

Powerstock Forest Park
Forest trail and picnic site, Wootton Hill near Wootton Fitzpaine.

Puddletown Forest
Near Hardy's Cottage.
Two nature trails with picnic site.

Quantocks
Forest trail signposted from Nether Stowey.

Wareham
Wareham Forest Trail, off
minor road to Bere Regis.

Wells
Descriptive leaflet available
from Wells Museum for the
four trails nearby.

Wimbleball Lake
Brendon Hills.
Open all year.

Opening Times

The details given in the Additional Information are correct at
the time of publication, but are also subject to revision and
should be checked beforehand if there is any doubt. This is
particularly true for opening times at Bank Holidays. Most of
the sites listed close at Christmas and New Year, but are open
at Easter and all other Bank Holidays. This is not true of all
sites, and there are changes from year to year.

Transport

Rural transport to the outlying areas is often sparse unless
there is a sizable community to serve. Useful addresses of bus
companies are:

Badgerline Ltd
(for Somerset and Wiltshire
buses)
Badger House
Oldmixon Crescent
Weston Super Mare
☎ (01934) 416171

National Travel Ltd
Victoria Coach Station
London SW1 W9TP

Wiltshire and Dorset Bus Co
Salisbury Bus Station
Salisbury
☎ (01722) 336855

Walking

The Downs of Wiltshire and Dorset offer some of splendid
walks in rolling countryside, while the coastal areas range
from gentle paths to cliff tops with beautiful scenery. Many of
the Tourist Information Offices have books or leaflets detailing

recommended walks. Areas recommended for special beauty or interest are:

Brendon Hills
Wimbleball lakeside walks.

Dorset Coast Path

Dorset Downs Walk

Exmoor
Guided walks on Exmoor, details from the National Park Information Office at Dulverton.

Lyme Regis
The Golden Cap Estate has 15 miles of footpaths.

Minehead
Signposted walks to Dunster and Watchet.

Purbeck Hills
From Swanage to Corfe Castle over Nine Barrow Down.

Quantock Hills
A 9-mile ridge walk from West Quantoxhead.

Severn to Solent Walk

Somerset & North Devon Coast Path

Taunton Deane
A booklet on the walks is available from the local Tourist Information Office.

Two Moors Way
Northern section over Exmoor.

Wells
Nature trails at Ebbor Gorge, Cheddar Gorge, Somerset Levels, descriptive leaflets available from Wells Museum.

Wincanton
Leaflet available.

Many towns have town trail leaflets for self-guided walks, or guided walks with local experts leading the way. These often give historical details or local anecdotes that are not easily found by other means. Recommended town trails are:

Bournemouth
Guided town walk.

Bridport
See notice in the Tourist Information Office window for details of guided walks.

Dorchester
Town trail.

Marlborough
Town trail.

Salisbury
Town trail.

Weymouth
Town trail.

INDEX